Praise for *The Six Co*

The extent of our isolation and loneliness is tragically evident everywhere—and this beautifully written and carefully crafted book is a powerful antidote. Its simple practices offer the experience promised to us in the Bible that "where two or three are gathered in my name, there am I among them" (Matt. 18:20). Here is a path forward to the connectedness that can bring us out of terrifying isolation and into the experience of the sacred. I am very grateful that this book exists!

MARGARET WHEATLEY
Author of ten books, including *Leadership and the New Science* and *Who Do We Choose to Be?*

In a world desperately in need of connection, this book is the tool we have been waiting for. As a counselor, I see people longing for heart connection but lacking the tools for conversation. This book is a life-changing treasure chest full of practical tips to help us find a community that has depth and connection. Heather's writing feels like having coffee with a friend who is training us how to have meaningful relationships through the beautiful art of conversations.

JENNIFER HAND
Author of *My Yes Is on the Table* and podcast host of *Coming Alive Conversations*

I smiled many times reading this book; I could feel Heather's loving, curious, and enthusiastic energy shine through—she walks the talk! The best of life is indeed conversation, and Heather shares powerful mindsets and frameworks to add vitality, meaning, and connection to any and all of our conversations.

GEORGIE NIGHTINGALL
Founder of Trigger Conversations (a London-based human connection organization)

As a communication professor, I am constantly looking for resources and guides to help my students better engage in the process of relationship building. I am so excited about *The Six Conversations* by Heather Holleman. At a time when people are increasingly divisive, we need more trained communicators who are willing to build bridges.

HEATHER THOMPSON DAY
Author of *It's Not Your Turn*

When you read Heather Holleman's new book, *The Six Conversations*, you will see how she not only knows how to connect with students, she also helps them grow in their ability to connect with others. And now Heather is doing the same for you and me! Before you finish reading *The Six Conversations*, you will be buying additional books to give to your friends and family to help them grow in their ability to connect with others too!

BOB TIEDE

Blogger at LeadingWithQuestions.com; author of five popular books, including *Great Leaders ASK Questions* and *Now That's a Great Question*

If there was ever a time this book was needed, it is *now*! We live in a social media world filled with distractions, isolation, and incivility. In this book, Dr. Heather Holleman intervenes to revive the art of conversation that leads to deeper connections, something all of us desire. Our world desperately needs faith-filled communicators who can connect and engage with others, no matter their background, lifestyle, or beliefs. This book is life-changing!

JEN BENNETT

Assistant Professor of Communication; host of the *She Impacts Culture* podcast; author of *#BeWorthFollowing: How to Be Different and Influence People in a Crowded Social World*

As codirector of the Winsome Conviction Project, I've seen many conversations blow up with voices raised and relationships strained, or even severed. I've also seen some amazingly civil and compassionate conversations between people who deeply disagree. What's made the difference? How much we think about not just *what* we want to say, but *how* to say it. Dr. Holleman's book is a perfect tool for helping us understand how to develop a loving mindset heading into a conversation and how to maintain it when things get heated.

TIM MUEHLHOFF

Professor of Communication, Biola University; author of *Winsome Conviction: Disagreeing without Dividing the Church*

We are living in times of strife and deep division. Our inability to hear and connect with others keeps us isolated and lonely. This is true on a national scale as well as within communities and in homes. Dr. Heather Holleman offers an accessible way for all of us to learn the skill of deeper connection through meaningful conversation. This is a worthwhile and practical book that I will return to over and over.

VIVIAN MABUNI

Author of *Open Hands, Willing Heart*; podcast host of *Someday Is Here*

THE SIX CONVERSATIONS

Pathways to

Connecting

in an Age

of Isolation

and

Incivility

HEATHER HOLLEMAN

MOODY PUBLISHERS

CHICAGO

© 2022 by
HEATHER HOLLEMAN

Unless otherwise indicated, all Scripture quotations are from the ESV® Bible (The Holy Bible, English Standard Version®), copyright © 2001 by Crossway, a publishing ministry of Good News Publishers. Used by permission. All rights reserved. The ESV text may not be quoted in any publication made available to the public by a Creative Commons license. The ESV may not be translated into any other language.

Scripture quotations marked (NIV) are taken from the Holy Bible, New International Version®, NIV®. Copyright © 1973, 1978, 1984, 2011 by Biblica, Inc.™ Used by permission of Zondervan. All rights reserved worldwide. www.zondervan.com The "NIV" and "New International Version" are trademarks registered in the United States Patent and Trademark Office by Biblica, Inc.™

Published in association with Tawny Johnson of Illuminate Literary Agency, www.illuminate literary.com.

Emphasis to Scripture has been added by the author.

Edited by Pamela Joy Pugh
Interior design: Puckett Smartt
Cover design: Erik M. Peterson
Author photo: Rebecca Desmarais / My R.A.D. Pics

Library of Congress Cataloging-in-Publication Data

Names: Holleman, Heather, author.
Title: The six conversations : pathways to connecting again in an age of
   isolation and incivility / Heather Holleman.
Description: Chicago : Moody Publishers, 2022. | Includes bibliographical
   references. | Summary: "The heart of this book is to connect people in
   loving community. Heather shows us how to embrace the Four Mindsets of a
   Loving Conversation and the Three Fresh Goals for Conversation. Readers
   are equipped with effective questions and action steps to implement in
   any situation-both personally and professionally"-- Provided by
   publisher.
Identifiers: LCCN 2022014736 (print) | LCCN 2022014737 (ebook) | ISBN
   9780802429391 (paperback) | ISBN 9780802473639 (ebook)
Subjects: LCSH: Conversation--Religious aspects--Christianity. |
   Interpersonal relations--Religious aspects--Christianity. | BISAC:
   RELIGION / Christian Living / Personal Growth | RELIGION / Christian
   Living / Leadership & Mentoring
Classification: LCC BV4597.53.C64 H65 2022 (print) | LCC BV4597.53.C64
   (ebook) | DDC 241/.672--dc23/eng/20220627
LC record available at https://lccn.loc.gov/2022014736
LC ebook record available at https://lccn.loc.gov/2022014737

Originally delivered by fleets of horse-drawn wagons, the affordable paperbacks from D. L. Moody's publishing house resourced the church and served everyday people. Now, after more than 125 years of publishing and ministry, Moody Publishers' mission remains the same—even if our delivery systems have changed a bit. For more information on other books (and resources) created from a biblical perspective, go to www.moodypublishers.com or write to

Moody Publishers
820 N. LaSalle Boulevard
Chicago, IL 60610

3 5 7 9 10 8 6 4

Printed in the United States of America

CONTENTS

FOREWORD

IT'S TIME WE TALKED MORE about how to love others well through our conversations. The good news is that I've never met one person who didn't want to grow in the art of conversation! Think about that feeling of warm connection after a truly great conversation. When was the last time that happened to you? How would your friends, coworkers, spouse, children, or others in your life rate your conversational skills? Wouldn't you enjoy knowing what questions to start and then continue asking to arrive at a place of meaningful connection? Or think about those stale, awkward encounters when you simply don't know what to say in a conversation. How would you like to never have to endure that nervous silence again?

This book is your guide to have better conversations, whether on a first date, in line at the grocery store, or with a friend or spouse you've had for a long time. Heather Holleman spends most of her time thinking deeply and studying the research about helping others connect well. In her college writing classroom at Penn State, Heather has become known for building authentic community through strategic questions for over a decade. With the epidemic of loneliness on college campuses, Heather knows that connecting people through meaningful conversation serves as a timely intervention.

Don't be deceived by the seeming simplicity of this book. Heather combined her expertise in rhetoric, study of social science research, and carefully thought-through biblical theology to write each sentence. With her expertise, she offers us this book as a conversation tool kit: this is the practical book we need to diagnose what's going wrong in our conversations to then repair and enliven them. As our happiness and the success of our marriages, family and work relationships, and friendships depends in part upon connected conversations, Heather's book provides the foundation and skills to talk to anyone in a meaningful and mutually beneficial way. Much like *The 5 Love Languages*, which offered readers five ways to express love to others (and understand their own love language), *The Six Conversations* gives you six categories of human connection in conversation you can immediately implement in any conversation. As loneliness increases and division runs rampant in our neighborhoods and churches, this book offers fresh hope that we can love each other again in our conversations.

GARY CHAPMAN, PhD, author of The 5 Love Languages series

A CONVERSATION REVIVAL

The best of life is conversation.

—Ralph Waldo Emerson

THIS BOOK REFLECTS one of the deepest passions of my heart: to connect people in loving community. Whether you're a student or you're further along in life and longing for a warm relationship with your spouse, dating partner, children, friends, in-laws, grandchildren, co-workers, clients, students, people in your neighborhood (or all of the above!), or simply wishing to improve your conversation skills in general, this book will help you have the kind of conversations that provide the foundation for well-being and joyful connection with others.

I've been investigating the research on happiness and well-being for years, not only for my own mental health and spiritual practice, but also because I care deeply about helping others thrive in my home, neighborhood, and classroom. I also regularly train others how to talk about their faith, and I quickly discovered a vital first step: before people can talk about their spiritual lives, they want to know how to have better conversations in general.

And we've lost that skill. We don't know how to talk with each other.

> "Warm, intimate relationships are the most important prologue to a good life."

Students regularly ask me how to improve their relational connections in their world that's now so dependent on texting, meme-sharing, inciting tweets, snapchats, and TikTok trends. They say things like, "Nobody talks anymore. They share Tik-Toks, but they don't *talk*." More recently, during a study from Cru, a parachurch organization, on understanding today's college student from February 2021, a student confessed that her generation "doesn't really know how to have a real conversation anymore."

Every semester at Penn State, dressed in my signature teaching outfit of a cardigan, plain T-shirt, black pants, and burgundy loafers, I stand in front of my advanced writing students after sharing the astonishing results of *The Study of Adult Development*, also referred to as the Harvard Grant Study—the longest research study ever conducted (and it's still ongoing). This research aims to answer a question we all care deeply about: *What is the single most contributing factor to a happy life?*

I pause and adjust my glasses. I sip coffee and wait. "What do you think? Is it more money? Is it accomplishments? Luxurious experiences? Fame? Whirlwind romance?" I watch their faces as I reveal the results as stated by the lead researcher himself. Dr. George Vaillant reports, "Warm, intimate relationships are the most important prologue to a good life."[1]

And then students inevitably ask this question: "How do we get those—those warm relationships?" I peer into their eyes. Are they really that lonely? Is it really as bad as I think it is for them?

Is It Really That Bad?

I immediately recall the studies on the epidemic of loneliness on college campuses and how Harvard's research on loneliness tells me 61 percent of young people today report feelings of "serious loneliness"[2] (only heightened by the COVID-19 pandemic) and the alarming results of the 2018 Cigna health study of over 20,000 US adults:

Nearly half of Americans report sometimes or *always feeling alone* (46 percent) or left out (47 percent).

One in four Americans (27 percent) rarely or *never feel as though there are people who really understand them.*

Two in five Americans sometimes or *always feel that their relationships are not meaningful* (43 percent) and that they are isolated from others.

One in five people report they rarely or *never feel close to people* (20 percent) or feel like there are people they can talk to (18 percent). . . .

Only around half of Americans (53 percent) have daily meaningful in-person social interactions, such as having an extended conversation with a friend or spending quality time with family.

Generation Z (adults ages 18–22) is *the loneliest generation* and claims to be in worse health than older generations.[3]

The Cigna research resounds in my mind when I see a group of students and imagine their thoughts: *I always feel alone; I'm left out; nobody understands me; I'm isolated with no good relationships; I don't have people to talk to; I don't have meaningful conversations; my health is suffering as a result.*

It's time for a global conversation revival to help quell the epidemic of loneliness revealed by, not just the United States, but also by Britain,

Switzerland, and Germany, who all work to tackle the epidemic of loneliness in their countries,[4] just as Japan most recently appointed a Minister of Loneliness due to the horrifying increase in suicide rates.[5]

I had to do something. As a college professor and expert community builder, I aim to intervene in the crisis, not just on the college campus, but also within places closer to home: around our dinner tables, within our neighborhoods, and next to the workplace coffee cart. As I sat worrying over my own campus, I received an alert about a new research study on "diseases of despair" in my state of Pennsylvania. The research revealed that diseases of despair—suicidal thoughts and behavior and alcohol and substance abuse—stem from a key theme of loneliness and lack of social support. The report reads that a major factor among three others "was a deteriorating sense of community. Participants discussed fragmentation over the last several decades that has led to rising isolation and distrust, and a lack of neighborly support."[6]

What Can We Do?

This book reveals to you a strategy I've learned that works to achieve warm relationships. It's a strategy and accompanying skill set rooted in research, framed by the wisdom literature in the Bible, and implemented immediately and easily to improve your friendships, romantic partnerships, family relationships, and work life.

The question hangs in the air in my classroom: *Dr. H! How do we get those warm relationships?*

"I promise I'll help you," I tell them. "It's easy. You can start tonight on your date, at your club, or with your roommate."

This book is the help I promised those students. It offers the missing ingredients—how we move from knowing someone's name to vital warm relationships—by presenting the linchpin: good questions, stemming from interpersonal curiosity (along with three other mindsets you'll learn in chapter 1), designed to foster intimacy. You'll learn these Four Mindsets along with the Six Conversations we'll discuss in chapter 8, a title that emerged on the morning my husband, Ashley, stepped into the bedroom and burst out: "It just hit me! Why can't we just train people to think of conversations in six categories based on what it means to be a human made in the image of God?" He was frustrated—but also inspired and motivated—by the evangelism training he presented nationally within our mission organization. While the training went well, he realized he missed something. The training people most wanted didn't involve more theology or more inspiration; the training people most wanted was *how to have a loving conversation.* Ashley continued with his hands in the air, exasperated: "How can we talk about our spiritual lives if we don't know how to connect—or worse, if we don't even care to be curious about other people? How can we enter into people's lives in loving, joyful, positive ways? It has to start with good questions."

I pulled out my journal and pen as Ashley paced around the room. "It's just six categories. Think about it. You start a conversation with someone, right? Anyone: family, friend, coworker, stranger. Then what? Nobody knows what to ask next. But what if they knew they could ask a question in one of these six categories? It's so easy!"

Why Six Conversations?

This book offers six essential categories of conversational questions once you learn the Four Mindsets for a Loving Conversation along with the Three Fresh Goals of Conversation (chapter 4). They allow you to run through a mental framework to know *what to ask* when launching into a conversation, *where to go next* when you feel stuck, and *where to linger* as you sense your conversation partner enjoying and responding to your category of questions. This framework reflects six categories of human experience:

Social: the full range of all our social interactions
Emotional: how we feel about ourselves and our experiences
Physical: our bodies and the physical space around us
Cognitive: what we think about and what we are learning
Volitional: our choices that give us a sense of control and authority
Spiritual: our soul and the unseen spiritual world around us

Each category's questions provide easy and memorable ways to build and maintain warm connections in conversation. If you're wondering why questions matter so much, answer these questions:

When was the last time someone asked you a question that invited you to truly open your heart in conversation?

How close do you feel to your spouse? Your children? Your best friends? How close do you feel to your neighbors and coworkers? Do you find you don't know how to draw people into conversation, and if you can, would you describe these conversations as "warm" and "connected"?

Have you ever been with another person, and this person failed to ask you one meaningful question about your life?

Have you ever been with another person, or in a group, and found that you felt more alone than ever because nobody truly connected through a good conversation question?

Have you ever felt awkward and unsure where to go next in a conversation? Are you afraid of long silences when nobody knows what to talk about?

What about these statements below I've heard from others?

I returned from a long trip. Not one family member or friend asked me a question about my time away.

Sometimes when I'm out with friends, I ask all the questions to keep the conversation going. Nobody ever asks me about my life.

I feel so lonely at school. Not one person asks me a personal question.

I feel lonely in my own family. We don't really talk to each other.

I don't know how to talk to my spouse anymore. We are growing apart.

I want to tell others about what I most care about (my faith, my passions), but I don't even know how to begin a conversation with anyone.

A Conversation Revival

This book makes building and maintaining warm relationships easier, and it fosters the right mindset going into any conversation. Therefore, Part One lays the groundwork for what it means to have a loving conversation, and Part Two offers the practical skills you can apply immediately to improve any social interaction. At the time of this writing, the world is emerging from pandemic isolation, and in the US, we continue to reel from political division and racial and social unrest. As an associate teaching professor of rhetoric and composition at one of the top honors colleges in the United States, I also note the rise of incivility in our speech; we use social media to incite, rant, shame, and cancel. We find ourselves poised to now reconnect again in loving and healing ways. We might challenge one another to move away from inciting tweets and self-righteous rants and from a discourse rooted in the sharing of memes and surface level connection to *joyful and meaningful conversations.* **It's time for a conversation revival, and I invite us to reimagine better conversations—the kind for which we're all secretly longing.** When we begin to practice the Four Mindsets and the Six Conversations, we find our marriages, parenting, friendships, and work relationships become thriving places of hope, deep connection, and happiness. These connections now become sacred, joyful, and life-giving. Let's get started!

PART ONE

What Is a Loving Conversation?

CHAPTER ONE

THE FOUR MINDSETS OF A LOVING CONVERSATION

"You can't hate someone whose story you know."

—Margaret Wheatley, EdD, author and
community building expert

I'VE NEVER MET ONE PERSON who didn't wish they could have better conversations. When I begin teaching on this topic, students pay attention. They know their ability to connect well with others matters—not just to heal their chronic loneliness, alleviate relationship boredom, and improve the group dynamics in their clubs, but to also advance their professional goals. They also seek to repair relational damage with friends, family members, and romantic partners after a year that separated people based on political affiliations, views on the COVID-19 pandemic, and activity related to racial justice in the United States. The communication climate for so many has turned to suspicion, shame, hatred, and mockery. It's a world of being canceled and unfriended if you say the wrong thing. So many of us feel awkward and unsure as we emerge from isolation. Like my students, you might ask these questions: *How can I connect again with others? How can I feel close to this person? If my personal happiness depends on having warm relationships—like all the research shows—how can I become a better conversationalist to foster these connections?*

As a writing professor studying rhetoric and communication, I've investigated the social science research and analyzed conversation practices, positive communication, and the relational warmth so vital for well-being, health, and happiness. Like you, I want to grow in my conversation skills. I want to foster the relational connections that allow for true fellowship with others.

But how?

Let's start thinking about the best conversation you've had recently.

Think about the last conversation you had where you felt loved, understood, and connected to the other person or group involved. What was happening? Did you feel like the other person was *genuinely interested* in you? That they *liked* you? That they *cared* about your life? Did you feel like the other person *shared* in the conversation as well to create that closeness you've longed for?

When I can say yes to these questions, I know I've been in a great conversation.

Great conversations involve these essential elements of interest, liking, caring, and sharing. Great conversations cannot happen in the absence of one of these elements. And great conversations require cultivating the mindsets that continue to foster these elements. If I want great conversations, I need to know where I'm lacking and how I can develop my capacity for loving connection.

CULTIVATING THE FOUR MINDSETS OF A LOVING CONVERSATION

In simple terms, if I were to tell you the four most critical things to do to foster a warm and connected conversation, I'd say this:

Be curious
Believe the best
Express concern
Share your life

The technical research terms for each phrase above sounds much more academic: *interpersonal curiosity, positive regard, investment,* and *mutual sharing*. Essentially, these conversational mindsets and accompanying behaviors will build your friendships and teach you the art of positive communication—a form of conversation involving asking, complimenting, disclosing, encouraging, listening, and inspiring.[1] These mindsets embody what researchers on relational closeness call "closeness-enhancing behaviors" of "openness, attention, and involvement," as well as showing other people "dignity and respect."[2] We already identified these mindsets using different words when we thought about a great conversation we've had (interest, liking, caring, and sharing), so now let's see them in action as what you can do: *be curious, believe the best, express concern,* and *share your life*.

My neighborhood friend and Penn State colleague uses the Four Mindsets in nearly every conversation we have. We recently began walking together once a week. She's an engineering professor; I'm a writing professor. Her world is mostly math and technical problems; my world is vivid verbs and semicolons. She uses words I do not understand and delights in designing highly technical engineering problem sets for her students.

How do you create a warm relationship between an engineer and a writer? To make matters worse, she's my opposite: she's a runner; she loves adventure and travel; and she has a dog. I can't run. I like to stay home. And I have three cats. This conversation shouldn't work at all, right?

Here we go. I'm walking beside her (and her dog), and she

immediately asks about my latest writing projects, my teaching, and my children. *Genuine curiosity. She's so interested in things I'm interested in.* Next, she compliments me and tells me all the ways I'm inspiring her. *Positive regard. She likes me! She's already believing good things about me.* She's now asking me about my upcoming meeting and wants to brainstorm with me how I can achieve my goals. *Investment in my success. She's wanting me to win. She wants the best for me.* Then, she's vulnerable with me. She reciprocates when I ask about her engineering classes and her goals so it's a time of *mutual sharing*. She shares vulnerably about where she's struggling. An hour passes, and I feel the relational closeness and warmth that fuels us both for the rest of the week.

> *You don't have to wait to start connecting with others. You can start the conversation revival right now.*

I even find myself liking her dog.

Think again back to your favorite conversations. When was the last time you felt truly cared for because of the questions someone asked you about your life? When was the last time you felt that another person was looking out for your interests, wanting you to succeed, and figuring out ways to personally encourage you?

My students often look sad when I ask them this question. I know it's painful to feel alone and disconnected. But guess what? You don't have to wait to start connecting with others. You can start the conversation revival right now. You can develop the Four Mindsets yourself along with me, and we can start today to engage differently in conversations wherever we are. We all need friends to share our lives with. God made us relational beings, and with the latest research revealing our need for connection, we can grow in the areas of curiosity, positive regard, investment, and mutual sharing. And then, we can teach others.

Let's examine the Four Mindsets with more depth and analyze our own tendencies in each category.

Mindset One: Be Curious

In 1936, Dale Carnegie published *How to Win Friends and Influence People*, a book selling over 30 million copies to become one of the best-selling books of all time. Carnegie claimed something so simple about how to make lasting friendships. *Be genuinely interested in other people.* He famously wrote, "You can make more friends in two months by becoming genuinely interested in other people than you can in two years by trying to get other people interested in you."[3]

Simple enough, right?

I recently asked my teenage daughter if she has any friends who ask her about her life and seem to care about what happens to her. She talks about how rare this is, how nobody ever asks her questions about her life, and how, in a school of over 2,500 teens, she could only name *one person* who asks her personal questions. I then asked my college students the same question, and one student cried, "When I'm out with friends, they *never ask me one question* about myself."

> *Young adults long for someone to be curious about them, to draw them out and try to connect deeply through good questions.*

The class nodded in agreement.

In my classroom, we talk about the epidemic of loneliness especially in teens and college students—and how disconnected everyone feels.[4] Young adults long for someone to be curious about them, to draw them out and try to connect deeply through good questions, but instead, most people in their lives stay self-absorbed and self-involved.

When we get together with friends, besides talking about the news or the weather or simply monologuing about work or children, rarely will someone ask a good question about our lives. It leaves so many of us frustrated, isolated, and empty after spending significant amounts of time in meaningless interaction. If only we could foster curiosity about one another!

If I could pick the essential character trait for my children and students to develop, I'd choose that of *curiosity*. In fact, I also talk to both my undergraduate and graduate students about developing curiosity as a key professional skill. In particular, I mean *social* or *interpersonal curiosity*—the desire to know and understand more about other people. I read and think about curiosity because I've learned that people who don't desire to engage others about their lives—even at the most basic level of interest—stay disconnected, lonely, and perhaps even depressed. Psychology researcher Todd Kashdan feels so strongly about the value of interpersonal curiosity that he called it the "secret juice of relationships."[5] In fact, Kashdan argues that "if you take the fundamental things that people tend to want out of life—strong social relationships and happiness and accomplishing things—all of these are highly linked to curiosity."[6]

At Penn State, I'm known as the "Name Game" professor because I ask a key attendance question in every class designed to invite everyone in the room (myself included) to share something meaningful about their lives (and learn one another's names). Why do I do this? As I encourage students to disclose information about themselves, and then begin to display curiosity about other people—even in just that brief moment of answering a personal question—the simple activity builds a sense of belonging, increases our positive mood, generates closeness, reduces prejudice, and enhances our creativity and productiveness.[7] I'll often ask the class, "What do you want to learn about each other today? What are you curious about?" They'll often choose a question from my list of 100 favorite questions (see the appendix). We love answering questions about the first song we played over and over again or about something we're celebrating. They love to talk about the best meal on campus (the spicy ramen) or the best class they've ever taken and why. Even questions like, "What are you looking forward to?" or "What are your weekend plans?" inevitably invite follow-up questions rooted in curiosity: How did you get those tickets? How did you become interested in that? Who else goes to that event with you?

Becoming More Curious: If you scan the research articles in both psychology, social science, and neuroscience, you'll learn about both the scope and benefits of becoming a curious person. Leading researcher on curiosity, Todd Kashdan, explains curiosity like this:

> Curiosity's immediate function is to seek out, explore, and immerse oneself in situations with potential for new information and/or experiences. In the longer term, consistently acting on curious feelings functions to expand knowledge, build competencies, strengthen social relationships, and increase intellectual and creative capacities.[8]

Essentially, curious people desire new information about others; they believe they will learn something important or meaningful. But how does one develop curiosity? How do we leave our homes to engage well with others about their lives?

1. **Get excited about all you'll discover.** Socially curious people love learning about others because they believe other people possess rich treasures of experiences, insights, and wisdom to offer in conversation. When we allow ourselves to feel curious about other people's lives, we essentially believe that we will discover something meaningful and valuable from this interaction. Additionally,

a curious person often has a humble, teachable heart—a heart set on discovering more about the person before them who is made in the very image of God. Imagine the person in front of you will offer wisdom and perspective because of their unique point of view. Psychologist and educator Mary Pipher reminds us how another person's individuality is a "tremendous gift to the world" because it is a "one-of-a-kind point of view on the universe."[9] Even more, consider how other people are hiding a treasure within them; it's our job to unearth that treasure—whether the treasure is how they see their world, what they know, or simply who they are in all their radiant beauty as children of God. What if you learn something that might change your life? What if they say something that unlocks a mystery for you? What if this person is the next step on your journey or vice versa? What if together you make a connection about something you would have never otherwise known? Sometimes I picture two people coming together in conversation like it's a chemical reaction. Something amazing will happen in that moment. Something's about to *catalyze* (great verb!).

2. **Invest in your own well-being**. As it turns out, curious people maintain "high levels of well-being," and curiosity serves as a key ingredient in a "pleasurable and meaningful life" as reported by Todd Kashdan in his research.[10] In an article titled "Why Curious People Have Better Relationships," UC Berkeley reports how curiosity helps us deal with rejection, makes us less aggressive, and helps our social life.[11] I've heard someone say, "It's hard to be mad and curious at the same time." I thought about this statement when I received an angry phone call from someone of a different political position who wanted to complain to me about all the people who disagreed with her. Instead of being riled up and letting her comments fuel my anger, I said, "I'm so curious. Tell me again the story

of why you're so angry. Remind me why this issue matters so much to you." Curiosity protected my own emotions in that moment and saved me from saying things in anger I might regret.

3. **Act as if you are curious.** Since curiosity fuels creativity and joy—not only in families and communities but also in the workplace—business leaders have taken a great interest in how to cultivate a posture of curiosity. One business leader reports how a colleague began her journey toward living in curiosity. She began to ask herself this question: "What would I say *if* I were curious?" This single question helped her build her curiosity.[12] Does this sound too simple to you? Maybe it even sounds disingenuous—to *pretend* to be curious. Well, it's a great technique to try, especially if you want to grow in conversational confidence: simply enter a conversation and let your mind role-play what a curious person would ask. Imagine you're a curious person who loves gathering information about others for the pure joy of understanding their lives. You can use any one of the Six Conversation categories in chapter 8 to begin your journey into interpersonal curiosity.

4. **Let yourself even fall in love.** Using questions fueled by curiosity will build connections to others, often with immediate results for not only friendship, but also for romantic connections. Perhaps you've heard of the famous *New York Times* article published in *Modern Love* called "To Fall in Love with Anyone, Do This."[13] In this essay, author Mandy Len Catron references relationship scientist Arthur Aron's study of how to make strangers fall in love using just thirty-six questions. Dr. Aron succeeds in generating relational closeness in a lab setting in only forty-five minutes, because of how the questions invite self-disclosure.[14] You can read Dr. Aron's list of questions in *Modern Love*; my favorites from his

list include these: What would constitute a perfect day for you? When did you last sing to yourself? What is your most treasured memory?[15] Not surprisingly, Dr. Aron's list of questions fits neatly into the six dimensions of what it means to be human.

So let's be curious.

Curious people build better relationships. Curious people experience greater well-being and pleasure. Curious people become more creative and less stressed out. And your curiosity just might lead you to romance.

3 TIPS FOR GROWING INTO AN INTERPERSONALLY CURIOUS PERSON

1. Begin a conversation with these words: "I'm so curious. Tell me about _____."
2. Make a list of people in your life you'd like to grow closer to. What are some things you'd like to know about them? Turn to chapter 8 on the Six Conversations and pull out your favorite questions from your favorite category.
3. Attempt to ask a question rooted in curiosity to every single person you encounter—even strangers—and see the effect it has on other people (and yourself!). At the end of the day, record the most surprising things you learned.

Mindset Two: Believe the Best

Without positive regard (believing the best), our attempts at curiosity won't make much difference. I've known people who act curious about my life for self-serving reasons; they want morsels to gossip about or ways to trap me in opinions they want to disparage. Or they just run through a list of questions because they are trying to connect out of duty or because it feels like a good leadership skill to ask a good question. Worse, I know they don't necessarily like me or wish to warmly connect; they want to talk for argument's sake. But when someone asks questions rooted in genuine interest from a position of love and respect, I love to open up to this person.

My marriage, parenting, and teaching rest on the foundation of this phrase *positive regard*—a term I borrowed from psychology—in particular Carl Rogers, who believed that the best way to help people is to first accept them just as they are without trying to change them, judge them, or shame them.[16] He noticed incredible transformation in clients when he simply said, "I accept you totally."[17] In simple terms, positive regard means you position yourself to respect, admire, like, and enjoy the person with whom you're in conversation. If you start from that point, you'll find that conversation blossoms; people want to share their lives with you. They feel safe, understood, and cared for in your presence. Positive regard changes conversation, and it changes people within those conversations. Research studies even suggest that positive regard from coaches and teachers creates more confidence and motivation from athletes and students;[18] positive regard helps others persevere through difficulty and perform better.[19] Not surprisingly, in the workplace, positive regard among coworkers enhances job performance and even makes employees better citizens.[20]

We naturally offer positive regard in our parenting when we say things like, "Nothing you could ever do would cause me to love you less or cause me to stop loving you. You can tell me anything." But in a marriage, we often don't start from this point. We instead begin from a point of suspicion, believing the worst, criticism, nagging, or blame. A marriage counselor once offered her best advice for the success of any marriage: *believe the best about your partner.* I was the type of newlywed who kept a record of all the ways I felt like my husband wasn't meeting my needs. I would recall ways he let me down or chores he hadn't finished. My toxic mindset made our marriage terrible *until I began conversations by believing the best about him*—and showing my positive regard with compliments and high praise. Twenty-two years later, our marriage has flourished. Just as I never judge or shame him, he shows me positive regard as well.

In our work lives, we often function as if others need to earn our respect and our time. When I applied the principle of positive regard in my classroom, I told students my teaching philosophy: *I am with you and for you. Nothing you do in this class will change my positive opinion of you, and I will work hard to assist you in your professional goals.* Not surprisingly, our classroom community flourished and students began to write more vulnerably and powerfully with an authentic written voice. My five-year research into the study of shame allows this kind of classroom; people can do bad things (guilt), but they are not bad people (shame).

In day-to-day interactions, especially with young people, positive regard matters most of all for helping others experience true belonging. In *Belonging: Reconnecting America's Loneliest Generation*, researchers argue that "accepting young people without judgment is an essential condition for belongingness to occur" and that this belongingness is "the state or feeling of connectedness that arises when seen, known, and accepted by another."[21]

Finally, believing the best about people is a way of extending God's grace to people. Grace refers to the unmerited favor of God; He loves us despite what we do. As a Christian, I know that God continues to bless me and love me in the midst of my bad choices or failures. When I extend this mindset toward others, I reflect God's grace to them.

When I'm having trouble choosing to believe the best about someone because of their actions or attitudes that I may find morally reprehensible, I try to think of what this person was like as a child. I remember to discover the story behind why this person feels or acts as they do. Then I find myself overcome with compassion rather than condemnation.

How does someone know you believe the best about them unless you tell them? As you choose to believe the best, practice complimenting people in your life and telling them simple things such as, "I really enjoy talking to you."

3 TIPS FOR BELIEVING THE BEST ABOUT PEOPLE

1. Try to recall or imagine a person who loves you unconditionally—like a parent or grandparent. Picture how his or her face lights up when talking to you. Picture that loving presence who invites you to share your life and talk about things that matter. Try to model this behavior as you talk to others. To remind you, imagine what it feels like to enter into a conversation with someone who you feel judges you, who criticizes you, and who is looking for ways to put you down, improve you, or change you. Nobody wants to open up in an environment like this.

2. Begin a conversation like this: "I'm so happy to be talking with you. I really enjoy connecting with you." Offer compliments. Remember God's grace extended to you that you now radically extend to others. Recent research from the Yale Relationship Lab on expressing gratitude for a friend showcases how doing so increases the sense of relational closeness. In this study, participants were encouraged to verbally thank a friend for something he or she did, express gratitude over a positive memory of that friend, or verbally indicate something you appreciate about your friend.[22]

3. Make a list of the people in your life you care most about. Write down several things you admire and respect about them. This will foster a mindset of positive regard, and it will give you suggestions for how to compliment them the next time you see them.

Mindset Three: Express Concern

If you're learning to be curious about others and you've trained your mind to begin with positive regard, you'll find that conversations might still lack the warmth and meaning you're hoping for. What's missing then is *investment*. Investment means you're interested in the outcome of what a person shares with you, and you express concern about their lives. You're devoting time and energy because you care about what happens to the other person. You're *invested* in their lives. You're listening in order to support, encourage, and inspire. Investment also implies a gain on the behalf of both parties. You link their success with your success, their failure with your failure, their sadness with yours. Investment is a form of support that moves beyond empathy; it's a willingness to "carry each other's burdens," a biblical phrase written in the book of Galatians. Investment refers to a part of positive communication that focuses on "common good" (when one person thrives, we all thrive) and "supportive" interaction.[23]

In a recent study on how people form "mutually responsive close relationships," researchers stated that "an optimal relationship starts with it being a relationship in which people assume a special responsibility for one another's welfare."[24] I'm learning when I engage in loving conversations with others, communicating investment makes all the difference in the quality of connection. Therefore, we can express concern about what someone is going through. Consider this: your friend might be genuinely curious about you and like you, but if he doesn't really care about the information you're sharing with him, you won't feel the connection and warmth you otherwise could.

When I recently applied for a new career opportunity, I shared the information with a few friends. I found that the only friend I wanted to talk to about this new direction in my life was the one who showed true concern. She'd call, text, or offer to go on a walk and ask, "Okay, what's happening with that opportunity? What's the latest? How are you feeling? I'm so excited for you. Tell me everything about it." This same friend asked me about my latest book contract and celebrated me so much it felt like it was *her* book contract, not mine.

Professionally speaking, I've had supervisors who casually ask about my work with curiosity and perhaps even positive regard, but they show no genuine concern. It doesn't really matter to them what happens to me. But I have one boss who shows sincere investment in my career: she inquires about my research, my writing, my contract negotiations, and my opportunities *as if they were her own*. She talks about my future as if it were somehow tied up in her own success. Guess which supervisor I most want to perform well for, who motivates me most of all, and who makes me feel valued?

> Investment is a way to live communally and joyfully so that you genuinely celebrate with others just as you would mourn with them.

Colleagues often ask me why I tend to enjoy perfect attendance in my classroom and why students visit in office hours and stay connected with me relationally even twenty years later. I believe the secret is *investment* and how I've learned to express concern about what's happening in my students' lives—whether they have an interview, a parent battling cancer, a breakup, or anything important they're going through.

Expressing concern is perhaps the hardest skill of all because it involves the wisdom to know what to do and how to help with the information someone shares with you in conversation. Investment doesn't mean to take on everyone's problems as your own, but it does mean you position yourself to support others as you can, to care about them, and to imagine an interconnectedness with their lives. It's a way to live communally and joyfully so that you genuinely celebrate with others just as you would mourn with them.

3 TIPS FOR EXPRESSING CONCERN

1. Consider that someone else's success is tied to your own and that you are interconnected. Begin a conversation like this: "What's happening with that challenge or opportunity? I'm so excited to hear what's happening there. Update me on your good or bad news. I'm here to support you." My daughter's kindergarten teacher taught all the students to make a "happy comment" if someone shared good news. Think about making happy comments, comforting comments, and supportive comments as someone invested in another person's life. If you are unsure what to do or say, a person who is invested in another person might ask, "How do you like others to show their support to you?" You can also tell people the kind of support you are able to give. When friends are struggling, I ask, "How can I best support you today? Would you like a walk, a phone call, a coffee delivery, or a meal?"

2. Find out what the people in your life are concerned about. What are their major stressors? What upcoming decisions loom? What are they worried about?

3. Discover what the people in your life are celebrating or what good news they have. You'll find in the Six Conversations chapter many ways to unearth information that you can express concern about—whether good news or challenges.

Mindset Four: Mutual Sharing

You can ask questions rooted in interpersonal curiosity, from a position of positive regard, and express great concern, but at that point, you might feel more like an interviewer or even a therapist. How do these skills lead to the warm relationships so vital for well-being? The last missing factor? Mutual sharing. In *The Art of Positive Communication*, professor of Applied Communication Julien Mirivel tells us the seven behaviors needed in a great conversation. Besides greeting, asking questions, complimenting, encouraging, listening, and inspiring, great conversations involve disclosing personal information.[25]

I'll admit it: I'm the worst at this. I'm great at asking questions (I'm naturally curious about other people). I'm great at believing the best (I saw how it saved my marriage). And I'm growing in the art of investment and showing concern as God helps me truly love other people better. But I hesitate to share vulnerably. I like to stay in control of a conversation. I like to avoid any situation where I reveal too much about myself. I'm the type of friend who regularly hears this statement: "Hey! You're asking all the questions. My turn! I want *you* to share now."

Maybe it's pride. Maybe it's the fear of shame. Maybe it's simply a form of control. Or maybe I've been in too many conversations where I do share something only to have the other person immediately make the conversation all about them. Worse, I've been in too many conversations where the other person spouts out advice or ways I need to improve. Have you experienced this? Sometimes our conversational histories have shut us down, but consider how vital disclosing personal information is to relational warmth. It might feel risky and even scary. Your heart might beat a little faster with the mere thought of talking about yourself with another person. But I promise you'll gain all the benefits of warm relationships if you commit to grow in this conversational skill.

To grow in the mindset of mutual sharing, I work hard to disclose personal information. I'll answer the question from the 100 favorites along with my students as honestly as I can. I am also learning to think about whether or not there's a *balance of sharing* in my conversations. Has my conversation partner shared about their life vulnerably? Is it now my turn to do so? Then, I practice sharing my life. As a part of positive regard, consider that sharing your life is a gift to another person. Do we not believe that another person is worthy of this gift? Do we stay guarded and silent because we secretly believe another person isn't wise enough, kind enough, or important enough to know us? Are we waiting for another person to somehow earn the right to our friendship?

Ouch. I'm like this. I close my heart to people all the time, but I'm learning to grow in the area of sharing my life with others.

Just recently, I endured an emergency kidney stone surgery. When neighbors came by to drop off soup and express concern, I thought about how to answer the inevitable question, "How are you doing?" Instead of saying "Fine. I'm fine!" I chose to share vulnerably about my fear and my pain. I even let myself cry in front of one couple who immediately asked if they could pray for me in that moment. I felt so loved and so connected to them. When my students asked me the next week all about this emergency surgery, I told them how I *really* felt. I then asked if any of them had ever endured something like my experience. That day, we connected like real humans about the pain our bodies go through throughout our lives.

When I forget to share my life, I remember a key research study on "closeness enhancing behaviors" in conversation. According to the research on the three best strategies to create relational closeness, *openness*—the "willingness to share personal information" and not "withhold private information" matters deeply.[26] The other two behaviors—attention and involvement—relate to the mindset of *investment*. When we're invested and share our lives, we'll find we're on our way to truly meaningful conversations with others.

3 TIPS TO GROW IN SHARING YOUR LIFE WITH OTHERS

1. Think of how you relate to a person's situation. In conversation, you can find common ground with others after they've

had ample time to share. Instead of interrupting to immediately discuss your life, wait until they have shared thoroughly. You might even ask, "Is there more to that story?" to make sure others have finished sharing what they want and need to share. Then it's your turn. You can begin to share your life by saying, "I can relate to that. In fact, I recently . . ." If that feels too self-focused and not appropriate, remember you can talk about how another person's situation feels to you. You can express raw emotion with them by saying, "When you told me that, I felt so sad. I don't know what to say, but I'm so glad I'm here with you."

2. Consider topics on the subject of *you*. On any given day, develop the self-awareness to know three things you're struggling with, three things you're celebrating or happy about, and three upcoming decisions or areas of uncertainty. Discover your default conversation (what you tend to talk about and like talking about) from chapter 9. Let your conversation partner know you love connecting over these topics.

3. Use the Six Conversations to think of categories of responding to and connecting to others. When it's your turn to share your life, you can begin with these prompts:

> *This reminded me about a similar interaction . . . (social)*
>
> *That made me feel . . . (emotional)*
>
> *You bring up a great point that made me think about my body or environment . . . (physical)*
>
> *Your story makes me wonder about . . . (cognitive)*
>
> *As you were talking, I began to think about this decision differently . . . (volitional)*

As you spoke, I remembered something about my faith that's helped me . . . (spiritual)

I'm still growing in the area of sharing my life. That's my greatest deficiency in the Four Mindsets. What about you? You might feel you want to grow in the areas of being more curious or more invested in other people. You might read this chapter and think of all the people you'd love to see with positive regard. As you finished this chapter (alone or in a group), rate yourself in the Four Mindsets of a Loving Conversation and begin challenging yourself to learn and practice new attitudes and behaviors in conversation.

FOUR MINDSETS INVENTORY

Circle the answer to each statement and take some time to answer the reflection questions.

Be Curious: I'm naturally curious about other people:

Rarely   Sometimes   Almost always

Reflect: Why do you think you feel this way? What happened to make you this kind of person? What's your next step in developing this skill? What resistance or hesitation do you have to this conversational skill?

Believe the Best: I tend to enjoy other people, easily admire them, and respect them:

Rarely   Sometimes   Almost always

Reflect: Why do you think you feel this way? What happened to make you this kind of person? What's your next step in developing this skill? What resistance or hesitation do you have to this conversational skill?

Express Concern: I have a hard time genuinely caring about what happens to other people:

Rarely   **Sometimes**   **Almost always**

Reflect: Why do you think you feel this way? What happened to make you this kind of person? What's your next step in developing this skill? What resistance or hesitation do you have to this conversational skill?

Share Your Life: I love to share my life with other people:

Rarely   **Sometimes**   **Almost always**

Reflect: Why do you think you feel this way? What happened to make you this kind of person? What's your next step in developing this skill? What resistance or hesitation do you have to this conversational skill?

If you're anything like me, you might still have some resistance or hesitation in your heart about the Four Mindsets. You might have questions about your personality and how to apply this book to your unique situation. But, if you're being honest with yourself (as I'm learning to be), we both know we long for close, meaningful relationships. And we truly want to become happier and more fulfilled people. While relationship science continues to advance the truth that we foster close relationships by becoming more open, more attentive to others, and more involved in their lives,[27] you might want to embed this book—not only in science and data, but through what the

Bible has to say about building healthy relationships. As you read on, we'll look at conversations through a theological lens to inspire you to grow into the kind of person who regularly commits to starting and continuing loving conversations.

CHAPTER TWO

A THEOLOGY OF A LOVING CONVERSATION

Do nothing from selfish ambition or conceit, but in humility count others more significant than yourselves. Let each of you look not only to his own interests, but also to the interests of others.

—Philippians 2:3–4

PENN STATE RECENTLY HIRED ME to develop an advanced writing course for the Schreyer Honors College—one of the top honors colleges in the United States. What I most admire about the Schreyer Honors College involves their commitment to ethical development and engaged citizenship. They wish to graduate student leaders who will truly make the world better. We therefore talk about living lives that function from the core values of integrity, of caring for the well-being of others, and of deeply including others—especially those from different cultures, backgrounds, and abilities. We also talk about how to dialogue well with others—not just in our writing, but also in all our interactions.

Essentially, my job is to help students *love others well*.

But how? And why? Where do these values of caring and inclusion come from, and why would I believe so strongly in advocating for them? My Christian tradition provides the perfect framework for how I approach what it means to care for, include, and ultimately love others, especially at the basic level of conversation. We can learn from this tradition even if we come from a different religious position. I often refer to the Bible as *wisdom literature* in the classroom because, within its pages, you'll learn how to live the wisest and best kind of life. Here, I offer a theology of a loving conversation rooted in the Bible. Your own religious tradition might add to and enhance what you read in the following paragraphs.

I'll confess this: Before I became a Christian, I was self-absorbed and self-involved. I was a child who talked way too much, or, to put it kindlier, I had "high articulation needs." My older sister and parents don't laugh about these memories; they agonize over them. If you ask them about how much I talked as a child, they'll close their eyes and step back as if trying to distance themselves from the terrible memory of my talking, like people shielding their eyes from the glare of the fiery sun. My mom will say, "You have no idea. You have *no idea* how much she talked."

I heard this nearly every day: "Heather, stop talking. Heather, *please, please, please* be quiet. Heather! Let someone else talk. If you don't stop talking, I'm going to go crazy."

The irony of all this talking is that I said much but connected little. I was like a little dog yapping around everyone's feet, begging for attention. I never learned how to use my words to love other people or engage them in warm conversations. Instead, I monologued, spewed, and yammered. I was the fool of Proverbs 18:2 (NIV) who "finds no pleasure in understanding but delights in airing [her] own opinions." To give you a final picture of my endless and pointless talking, I would talk *to the air*. As an eight-year-old, I'd pace around my backyard and recite the Gettysburg Address for fun. I didn't even need an audience.

And I was lonely. Deeply lonely. The kind of lonely where you stare out the window with tears streaming down your face because you know friends are out there but you cannot figure out how to make them.

And I was dysfunctional. When I realized I wasn't making any friends, I became a people-pleaser and used flattery and compliments to try to bait people into liking me.

And I was isolated. I eventually stopped talking so much and turned inward—to scribbling in journals and to writing book after book. My husband once joked that

> *"I don't belong here. I don't belong anywhere. I don't know how to feel connected to people. I don't know how to have a conversation that means anything at all."*

the reason I write so many novels is to invent people to spend time with. I laughed. He's not wrong.

I never seemed to learn how to truly connect in real conversation.

And I was awkward. I'd sit in a room, fiddle with the buttons on my sweater, reposition my glasses and think, "I don't belong here. I don't belong anywhere. I don't know how to feel connected to people. I don't know how to have a conversation that means anything at all."

Maybe you've felt this way. Maybe you have had tears in your eyes like I do now as I write this.

Lonely. Dysfunctional. Isolated. Awkward.

But then, Jesus entered in to rehabilitate how I spoke. That's right: I learned from the Bible *how to have a loving conversation*, and the Holy Spirit changed me so profoundly that if you knew me before I began my relationship with Jesus you'd be astonished at the change.

My journey begins with the deep conviction that came with

reading perhaps one of the most personally challenging passages of Scripture. You'll find it in the book of Philippians, a letter written by the apostle Paul to the Christians in the Roman colony of Philippi around AD 62. It's a letter that answers these questions: *How shall we live as good citizens in God's kingdom? What does spiritual progress look like? What is Christian maturity?*[1]

In the second chapter of this letter, Paul writes this:

> Do nothing from selfish ambition or conceit, but in humility count others more significant than yourselves. Let each of you look not only to his own interests, but also to the interests of others. Have this mind among yourselves, which is yours in Christ Jesus, who, though he was in the form of God, did not count equality with God a thing to be grasped, but emptied himself, by taking the form of a servant, being born in the likeness of men. (Phil. 2:3–7)

I remember reading this passage for the first time as a young woman. The words stung my heart. I saw myself for the first time: I didn't value others as more important or more significant than myself. I didn't look out for the interests of others. I didn't serve others or "empty myself" as Jesus did.

Instead of humility, I was prideful and superior as I spoke to others.

Instead of caring about others, I only talked about my own problems.

Instead of serving others with my words to encourage and comfort, I only served myself and thought about what I could gain from a conversation, not what I could lovingly give.

I thought carefully about Philippians 2 for years. In the Greek translation, when you count others as more significant than yourself, the verb means to *esteem exceedingly*. How would anyone know I esteemed them exceedingly if I didn't tell them in conversation? How could I change the disposition of my heart to adopt that key mindset of positive regard, of not only believing the best, but truly holding someone up in my mind as more important than I am? (This is one of those impossible tasks that makes the Holy Spirit real to me; only God can do this kind of work in a heart as self-centered and self-exalting as mine.) I began, by the power of the Holy Spirit at work to mature me, to see other people as royalty, as VIPs, as marvelous celebrities. Imagine how you'd behave in conversation if you met Her Majesty the Queen (yes, her proper title—I watch *The Crown*!). Imagine how you'd behave in conversation if you met your favorite celebrity or your favorite leader in any field. Imagine your excitement. Imagine the honor. Imagine what you'd ask them.

Now think of your neighbor who maybe annoys you. Maybe you'd never talk to someone like her. But wait. *Queen. Celebrity. Honored Guest.*

Think of your children like this. Your spouse. Your coworkers.

When I began thinking this way, the first noticeable change for me involved my interaction with my students. I even told them to look to their left and right and imagine the person beside them would one day become a global superstar or even a world leader. *How would that change how you treated them?* The exercise brought awkward giggles and uncomfortable shifting in seats, but I made the point: the person beside you is a treasure, a marvel, a storehouse of infinite potential. That day, we let others go first through the doorway. We let others be most important for once.

The second change came when people started to tell me how they felt around me. My colleague said, "You make people feel really special when you talk to them." I almost cried; I was so happy I was growing like this.

But it wasn't just the mindset of positive regard and choosing to value others before myself that built the groundwork for a loving conversation. Paul's words also deeply challenged me to ask better questions as I read, "Let each of you look not only to his own interests, but also to the interests of others." How would I know the interests of others if I didn't ask them? How else could I figure out what other people worry about or care about? I began regularly asking others about their current projects and major concerns. I asked what thoughts most occupied their minds. I would then imagine that this concern was now part of my own. I'd follow up in the coming days and ask about whatever we talked about. I'd look for ways I could encourage and help based on whatever my colleague, student, friend, or family member shared with me. My loving conversations, rooted in Philippians 2, became my primary act of service and the way I humbled myself to take on the nature of a servant.

As I continued to grow in the art of a loving conversation, I found so much biblical support for the Four Mindsets. Paul's command to discover the interests of others related directly to my becoming a curious person. Honoring others related to positive regard, and I found more commands to walk "with humility toward one another" (1 Peter 5:5). Paul even tells us to "outdo one another in showing honor" (Rom. 12:10). But what about the idea of investment and expressing concern about others? Paul tells us to "rejoice with those who rejoice [and] weep with those who weep" (Rom. 12:15) and to "carry each other's burdens" (Gal. 6:2 NIV). How would I know how to rejoice if I never ask about anyone's good news? How would I encourage and comfort others if I never ask about how they are struggling? And, most vitally, how could I continue in my past ways of selfishness if I ever wanted to uphold Jesus' command to love one another as He has loved me (John 15:12)?

Finally, consider the command to share our lives in verses like James 5:16: "Therefore, confess your sins to one another and pray for one another, that you may be healed." Telling other people how we're struggling invites this kind of prayer and healing. It's also a way to allow the often-quoted verse in Proverbs 27:17 to come about: "Iron sharpens iron, and one man sharpens another." Allowing this "sharpening" involves humility and the willingness to live vulnerably.

Paul seems especially passionate about the importance of sharing one's life as he penned the first letter to the Thessalonian church. He explains how delighted and ready he was to "share with you not only the gospel of God but also our own selves" (1 Thess. 2:8). I read this verse carefully as a young professional who wanted to build a philosophy of living as a teacher and friend. What would it mean to share my "own [self]" in the work God had called me to do as a teacher, mother, and friend? Sharing my life with others—my struggles, my hopes, my fears, and my victories—would forever become part of the art of conversation and a vulnerable risk I would choose to take over and over again.

If we look deeper into this idea of sharing "our own selves" from a biblical perspective, we might consider John 17 and the way Jesus prays for believers. Jesus prays that we would "be one" together just as the Father was in Him (v. 21). Think about the commands in Scripture to have "unity of mind" (1 Peter 3:8); to see ourselves as "one body" who are "members one of another" (Rom. 12:5); to understand our baptism into "one body—Jews or Greeks, slaves or free" (1 Cor. 12:13); and to live so interconnected that if someone "suffers, all suffer together" and if someone "is honored, all rejoice together" (1 Cor. 12:26).

The Bible presents us with a new model of connection: to see ourselves sharing our lives and becoming part of one another. The biblical writers lay this foundation for interconnection that social scientists prove over and over again in studies of relational closeness, most notably what researchers call "cognitive interdependence."[2] Groundbreaking reports from the leading researcher on relational closeness, Dr. Arthur Aron, explain how feeling close to others involves "including the other" in one's sense of self.[3] When we share our lives, together we find, according to the latest research on close relationships, "both individual and relational benefits" and more relational satisfaction.[4] Finally, in a review of the best research on relational science, scholars have noted "integration"—or interdependence that allows others to join together and share their lives—ranks as one of the key core principles in the psychology of close relationships.[5] Essentially, Jesus' desire for our interconnectedness reflects what the science of relationships now confirms. To put it simply, think of the famous quote from C. S. Lewis, who writes that all friendship comes from that moment when someone says, "What? You too? I thought I was the only one."[6] When you share mutually, you find the connection on which all great relationships depend.

> *"What? You too? I thought I was the only one!" When you share mutually, you find the connection on which all great relationships depend.*

I love how the Four Mindsets find their roots in the Bible's wisdom. When I read fascinating research about relational closeness that seems so technical and novel at first, I realize we've known these truths all along in the pages of Scripture. Ultimately, as we seek the goal of our Christian lives—to be conformed to the image of Christ—we must ask ourselves if Jesus Himself lived the Four Mindsets. Indeed, He did. First, while it might challenge us theologically to consider God as *curious* (since He knows all things), we do know that God "forms the hearts of all, [and] considers everything they do" (Ps. 33:15 NIV). We also know that God takes great interest in our well-being (Ps. 35:27).

Second, think about how God views us with positive regard

because we live under the righteousness of Christ; we're perfect in His sight (Rom. 3:22). God removes our sin from us and delights in us (Ps. 18:19); His "steadfast love surrounds" us (Ps. 32:10); and nothing can separate us from this divine love (Rom. 8:38–39).

Third, God expresses concern for our lives. He encourages us to allow Him to "daily bear our burdens" (Ps. 68:19 NIV) and to cast "our anxiety on him because he cares for [us]" (1 Peter 5:7).

Finally, God marvelously shares His life with us. The incarnation of God—who came to earth and made His dwelling among us—shows us God's desire to share and give up His very life to make a way for us to know Him. And He gives us the greatest gift of the Holy Spirit so we might experience union with Him. The Lord shares His thoughts with us as the Holy Spirit uses Scripture and prayer to communicate with His people. In Psalm 25:14, we read how "the friendship of the LORD is for those who fear him, and he makes known to them his covenant." God desires intimate connection with us, and Jesus gave up His life on the cross that we might be in conversation with the living God. Jesus Himself opened up and shared His sorrow in the garden of Gethsemane as told in Matthew 26:38. He says, "My soul is very sorrowful, even to death; remain here, and watch with me." That moment of vulnerability reminds me that God desires connection.

Conversations matter to God, and He models a perfect way to connect with others.

I want to grow in my ability to connect with others through loving conversations. I want to see conversations as a sacred space. Let's think about our next conversation as a way to honor others above ourselves, to value others above ourselves and take an interest in them, to encourage one another, to demonstrate kindness and compassion, and ultimately, *to love people*. When we do this, we reflect God's character.

In the next chapter, you'll learn to honestly assess your current conversational patterns and learn what pitfalls to avoid as you begin your own conversation revival.

CHAPTER THREE

OUR CURRENT CLIMATE

I feel the vacuum, the loneliness, the silence, the dehydration of the soul as people who want desperately to save our Constitution, country, and planet still wander the streets without even knowing how to say hi to one another.

—Sam Smith, American journalist

AS A COLLEGE PROFESSOR, mom of teens, and community member deeply concerned about Generation Z as the loneliest generation, I think about the double impact of two factors that create a perfect storm for disconnection from others: social isolation and the rise of incivility. We already know the research into loneliness—as explained in the introduction to this book—but what about incivility? I use the term "incivility" to capture a cultural moment in which we see a rise in mocking, shaming, and divisive speech that pits people against one another instead of fostering the belongingness so needed for our spiritual and emotional health.

When I tell people I'm writing a book on how to have better conversations, some of them immediately say, "Yeah! I want to learn how to win arguments better and handle all this disagreement. People are so ignorant! Make sure you write a chapter about that!" Or friends will agree we desperately need an intervention into the conversation about how we talk with one another. They tell me they've deleted Facebook and Twitter because the platforms have transformed into arenas of political arguments, rage, and cancel culture. Even seemingly innocuous social media apps—like neighborhood sites for sharing local news about garage sales and school delays—parade hateful comments disparaging a neighbor's political opinions or religious beliefs. My students at Penn State write papers about their fear of "cancel culture" that silences them from ever sharing an opinion. They also tell me how they block family members on social media because of their political ranting. No conversation feels safe.

Consider the spirit of our current climate. We cancel, block, rage, divide, and shame.

"So what happens to your conversations?" I ask. But I know the answer. As someone who studied shame cultures and the tormenting fear of shame, I know the cultural impact of public shaming. People shut down. They go into hiding. They lose an authentic self because they mediate their sense of identity through how everyone else is or will judge them.

While I wholeheartedly support the benefits of public accountability for wrongdoing and the power of political protest, especially the need to expose and condemn racism, sexism, and discrimination of all forms, I do think the current climate of communication often prevents real, personal transformation and social change. I know you might vehemently disagree with me. In fact, one of my best friends studies the sociology of race at Penn State, and she reminds me that people resort to outrage when there's no hope. They rage, demand, and humiliate others because they have been silenced for too long. And they riot because of pain and unimaginable suffering. She helps me understand both sides of the argument regarding our current conversational climate. Rage matters when you're fighting for systemic change. I agree. In fact, the revolutionary spirit that forged democracy, civil rights, and the freedom of speech that allows me to write this book reminds me how much it matters to stand up for what's right, to fight for the oppressed, and to seek justice everywhere. Jesus, remember, overturned tables in the temple to protest those running a business there. Protest and anger have their place.

However, *interpersonally*—how we connect with one another on a daily basis—we might think, then, that rage, mockery, disgust, anger, and shaming changes people's minds. Do we think we're endearing people to us by mockery and rage? Do we think people will open their lives to us and consider lasting personal transformation when we speak to them like this? Hardly. I think about churches now ripped apart, family members now estranged, and friends now parting ways because of perceived differences in beliefs or political opinions.

Here's the problem: When people expose themselves to a constant barrage of sensationalized, rage-filled posts on social media, it puts the brain in a *reactive*, rather than *responsive*, brain state. Conversations that constantly divide, stir up negativity, and incite others prevent the responsive brain state so vital for mental and social health. Reactivity prevents clear thinking and the ability to inhabit other viewpoints.

> *If we really care about changing people's minds, we have a much greater chance of engaging them if we stop mocking them.*

Psychologist and UC Berkeley research fellow Dr. Rick Hanson explains, "When people are in their reactive mode, their perceptual world narrows." Hanson contrasts this with a *responsive* mode: "When you are feeling positive emotion . . . your perceptual field broadens, and widens out, and therefore by definition, you're much more able to think and perceive and act in complex ways."[1] A responsive brain is a brain that's ready to learn and change. It's a brain that allows you to grow in multiple areas of well-being: "In responsive mode, you can experience gratitude, joy, contentment, or connectedness and are capable of intimacy, kindness, compassion, and love."[2] If we seek to create cultures of compassion and love, we might think more carefully about how we connect with others in loving, not divisive, ways. To put it simply, if we really care about changing people's minds, we have a much greater chance of engaging them if we stop mocking them.

Perhaps most troubling about the current conversational climate on social media involves what *Forbes* magazine recently exposed as our addiction to drama. We read from public health and behavioral science writer Nicole Roberts that "drama uses the same mechanisms in the brain as opiates" and "people can easily become addicted to drama. Like any addiction, you build up a tolerance that continuously requires more to get the same neurochemical affect. In the case of drama, this means you need more and more crises to get the same thrill."[3]

Essentially, we've addicted ourselves to controversy. We follow paths that lead to reactive brain states that play out in our face-to-face interactions. We're cued and increasingly conditioned to seek out and circulate drama, conflict, shaming, and bad news. We've normalized ourselves to conversations rooted in anger, complaint, and division. In fact, in their research on this "new normal" of speaking, Tufts University professors Sarah Sobieraj and Jeffrey Berry explain this incivility as the "outrage industry." In an interview about their research, Sobieraj explains how "outrage is . . . political speech and behavior involving efforts to promote emotional responses—especially anger, fear and moral indignation—from the audience."[4] The rise of this kind of speaking attempts to keep others focused on "melodrama, mockery . . . and impending doom."[5] Perhaps most alarming, Sobieraj and Berry explain how we observe and adopt a "unique brand of incivility" that is "not really about dialogue or information, but instead takes the form of a wildly entertaining verbal jousting match, with the victor of the day being the team that most effectively paints the other side as dangerous, misguided or inept."[6]

You might think this research simply showcases the rampant outrage in politics or on news shows and doesn't infect our personal interactions and daily conversations, but in fact, this "new normal" of outrage "[creates] barriers between people . . . and [makes] us less open to hearing" the ideas of others.[7] We become suspicious, afraid, and self-censoring because we fear both the judgments of others and their opinions, which we've been taught makes them dangerous, manipulative, or evil. So we stay quiet, find safe people who we think agree with us, and severely diminish our circle of who we might converse with at all. It's happened to me, and it's happening to you. If you're honest right now, you know you're avoiding people because of what you think they believe about the government, vaccines, climate change, or any issue confronting society.

I teach the art of persuasion and effective argumentation at Penn State. I tell my students the key to dialoguing effectively in important conversations involves listening, finding common ground, summarizing your conversation partner's viewpoint, and showing how your position ultimately benefits them. It's about connecting over core values. It's a rhetorical strategy rooted in *love.* They smile and nod their heads. Something rings true about this new way of connecting with others. I remind them how this kind of loving connection stands as a key professional development skill: knowing how to build rapport with others and foster a sense of togetherness with whom you're in conversation—no matter how different they are from you—impacts how you'll work on a team, in a staff meeting, and when connecting with stakeholders. I'm teaching skills of rapport building that now seem to go against the grain of their communication norms.

In my own life, I think about how the Bible defines "love," since my aim is loving conversation. In 1 Corinthians 13—the famous "love chapter" in the Bible (often quoted at weddings)—we read this: "Love is patient and kind; love does not envy or boast; it is not arrogant or rude. It does not insist on its own way; it is not irritable or resentful . . ." (vv. 4–5). I want to teach my students how to talk in humble, kind, and patient ways. I don't want them to live as the fool in Proverbs 12:16 where we read, "Fools shows their annoyance at once, but the prudent overlook an insult" (NIV). I want them to live honorable lives that bless others.

Loving in conversation is now countercultural. Consider Romans 12:14–16 where Paul writes these powerful words: "Bless those who persecute you; bless and do not curse them. Rejoice with those who rejoice, weep with those who weep. Live in harmony with one another. Do not be haughty, but associate with the lowly. Never be wise in your own sight." Where do you see this happening well? Where do you find people blessing their enemies? Where do you see humility? Before I speak, I think about whether my words build peace and connection (harmony) *or if they divide.* I want to live out Hebrews 12:14 (NIV) and "make every effort to live in peace with everyone."

As we resist the growing tide of incivility, we might also consider how our "new self" in Christ involves resisting behaviors that destroy warm connections and belongingness. In Colossians 3:8–15, we read about putting on this new self as a way to create profound unity in Christ. We read this:

> But now you must put them all away: anger, wrath, malice, slander, and obscene talk from your mouth. Do not lie to one another, seeing that you have put off the old self with its practices and have

put on the new self, which is being renewed in knowledge after the image of its creator. Here there is not Greek and Jew, circumcised and uncircumcised, barbarian, Scythian, slave, free; but Christ is all, and in all. Put on then, as God's chosen ones, holy and beloved, compassionate hearts, kindness, humility, meekness, and patience, bearing with one another and, if one has a complaint against another, forgiving each other; as the Lord has forgiven you, so you also must forgive. And above all these put on love, which binds everything together in perfect harmony. And let the peace of Christ rule in your hearts, to which indeed you were called in one body. And be thankful.

Can you imagine the Holy Spirit producing this kind of living in us? The kind where we walk around and speak to one other with *compassion, kindness, and humility*? Where we're *actively forgiving others*? Where we're no longer looking at what separates us but what unites us in Christ? In fact, as we "walk by the Spirit" as instructed in Galatians 5, we'll find our behaviors work to bring unity and peace. Think about it: in Paul's list of fifteen behaviors that signify the flesh (as opposed to godly, Spirit-filled behavior), *nine of them relate to interpersonal harm*. That's over 60 percent if you're a math person (I'm not!). Look at the list and see the kinds of behaviors we're warned about in verses 16–21. Paul writes:

But I say, walk by the Spirit, and you will not gratify the desires of the flesh. For the desires of the flesh are against the Spirit, and the desires of the Spirit are against the flesh, for these are opposed to each other, to keep you from doing the things you want to do. But if you are led by the Spirit, you are not under the law. Now the works of the flesh are evident: sexual immorality, impurity, sensuality, idolatry, sorcery, enmity, strife, jealousy, fits of anger, rivalries, dissensions, divisions, envy, drunkenness, orgies, and things like these. I warn you, as I warned you before, that those who do such things will not inherit the kingdom of God.

As I look around at the culture, I see the critical, faultfinding spirit we're warned about in Galatians. We see how, instead of loving one another, we provoke each other. We sit in the seat of scoffers (Ps. 1); we are not "quick to listen, slow to speak and slow to become angry;" we no longer believe that "human anger does not produce the righteousness that God desires" (James 1:19–20 NIV). I also consider Paul's instruction to young Timothy when he writes, "The Lord's servant must not be quarrelsome but must be kind to everyone, able to teach, not resentful. Opponents must be gently instructed . . ." (2 Tim. 2:24–25 NIV).

In essence, many Christians have become Pharisees who believe their religion exists to stand and expose the faults of others. It makes sense. Satan's primary weapon in the world is division, to oppose the unity so cherished by Jesus in John 17:20–23 where He prays repeatedly that we would "be one" and that we would "be brought to complete unity." The Holy Spirit, after all, is a spirit of unity (Eph. 4:3). If the Holy Spirit is a spirit of unity, and our unity with one another and Christ matters, then we might consider the origin of so much discord and fighting. What if our real enemy isn't who we thought?

When I was a young woman just learning how to walk with Jesus, I loved to gossip. I loved to stir up controversy. A wise pastor pulled me aside one day and told me something I will never forget. He said, "Did you know that Satan's name means, 'He who separates'? The translation of devil means to divide and to separate." Later, I learned Satan translates as "adversary," and devil as "slanderer"—or the Greek "he who divides," or more accurately, "scatters." That day, I began to ask myself if my words helped bring people together or not. Did my words divide others? Even more critically, I remembered how a mentor told me this stunning statement: "People are not the enemy. Satan is the enemy. You're fighting the wrong battle."

You're fighting the wrong battle.

To think better about changing the tone of our conversation, consider what changes when you enter a conversation. I recently asked my Penn State students a key professional development question about how they add value to any situation. I ask this question to prepare them for interviews and career fairs at Penn State. It's also a question designed to foster self-awareness and personal growth. I ask this:

"What changes when you enter a conversation?"

They pause and tilt their heads up to the ceiling to ponder.

"That's hard!" they protest. I'm asking them to see themselves from the outside and realize, at their best, they do bring something to the table. Still, they hesitate to speak.

"In other words, how do you add value to a situation? Do you bring energy, clarity, positivity, or accountability? Do you enter a conversation and add lightheartedness and gratitude? What changes with *you* present? What changes when you enter a room?"

It's a hard question, but I want them to think about how they're perceived and how they use their personalities and talents to uplift rather than harm. Certain people enter a conversation, and it's as if they bring a dark cloud with them. They suck the energy out of a room with their negativity, superiority, critical spirit, or self-absorption. They enter a conversation to divide, manipulate, mock, and shame.

Students realize their core values and key contributions as they offer up an answer. They might say things like this: *I bring clarity and strategic thinking. I bring humor so people don't take themselves too seriously. I'm the one bringing hope. I bring efficiency; I like to help people accomplish their goals quickly. I bring enthusiasm. I bring empathy. I bring a fresh perspective because of my background.*

What about you? What changes when you enter the conversation?

We can also add a layer of complexity to the question by asking ourselves what we *hope* to bring to a conversation and what we *fear* we actually bring to a conversation. You might think something like this:

I *hope* I enter a conversation to refresh and inspire people with my energy, but I *fear* I talk too much and overwhelm people. (This is my answer!)

I *hope* I enter a conversation to listen well and let others talk, but I *fear* I come off as aloof and disinterested. (The answer of one of my students who is rather quiet and introverted.)

I *hope* I offer good advice and strategic thinking, but I *fear* I come off as bossy or a know-it-all. (My neighbor's answer.)

What would you say? I hope I bring _____ to a conversation. But I fear I bring _____.

You might ask your friends or coworkers this question and ask them to give you honest feedback. Tell them you are working to improve your conversation skills and seek input to learn how others perceive you.

As both a Christian and rhetoric professor, I seek to rehabilitate conversations back to a biblical model rooted in something so beautiful and life-giving it will profoundly change how we connect with one another. I seek to forge a fresh path, a countercultural one, that draws up the ancient wisdom we've lost and desperately need to find again. This intervention into our current situation uses biblical language to remind us *what conversations are for* and *how to have them well.* In the next chapter, we'll answer a life-changing question: What's a conversation for? You don't have to accept this current cultural moment.

You can become a different kind of person who builds unity and learns how to warmly connect in loving ways with people whom you perceive as enemies or who think profoundly differently from you. Perhaps only then will we see the kind of changes in our communities for which we're hoping.

CHAPTER FOUR

WHAT'S A CONVERSATION FOR?

*Human conversation is the most ancient and easiest
way to cultivate the conditions for change—personal
change, community and organizational change, planetary
change. If we can sit together and talk about what's
important to us, we begin to come alive.*

—Margaret Wheatley, EdD, author and
community building expert

MAYBE WE'VE FORGOTTEN THE PURPOSE of a loving conversation.
Maybe the root cause of our conversational deficiencies stems from
an aimless start: we don't know how to connect with others or *why we
should*. And we don't know how to end an interaction with someone
in a way that brings the conversation to a joyful or meaningful close.
Think about this question: What is a conversation for?

3 FRESH GOALS FOR CONVERSATION

We want our conversations to create a loving, close connection. Before we delve into practical tools to help you begin and continue any

conversation, we might first consider the end goal of a conversation. What am I actually trying to *do* in a conversation? Is it more than just gaining information from someone? What does all this talking lead to?

Let's consider three conversational goals that help us meaningfully connect to others. So far, we've learned about the Four Mindsets and corresponding actions in a loving conversation (be curious, believe the best, express concern, share your life). Now we can add to these mindsets Three Fresh Goals for Conversations. I call these "fresh" goals because it's time to awaken the long-lost art of joyful, purposeful conversation. I root these goals in a biblical worldview, but these ideas also resonate with the social science research on how to build closeness and warmth in conversation. While many reasons exist for conversational goals (to learn, teach, warn, confront, seek assistance, network, etc.), three goals uniquely add value to others and help connect us in conversation. And, with these three goals firmly in mind, we avoid the Ten Pitfalls in Conversation which you'll discover shortly. Consider these Three Fresh Goals:

to mutually encourage

to aid personal growth

to marvel

The above list might surprise you. *Encouragement, growth, and marveling*? Why these three in particular? As I curated research articles, examined personal stories, and thought carefully about scriptural support for the goals of loving conversations, I find these three themes best summarize what happens in the best conversations. Think about your best conversations. The ones that leave you *feeling encouraged*, leave you inspired to *grow personally*, and ultimately lead you to *awe and worship*.

Close Conversations for Encouragement

Encourage one another and build one another up.—*1 Thessalonians 5:11*

When I was a college student working at a Christian summer camp, an older staff member left a bright yellow Post-it Note above my bunk. In the humidity of that North Carolina summer in the mountains, I read the words on that note that shaped forever how I thought about the way I talk to others. The staff woman wrote, "You are an encourager."

I stared at the note in wonder. Never in my life had someone named a spiritual gift in me. Never had I considered the special gift of grace—as listed in Romans 12 among the spiritual gifts—to serve as an *encourager* to other people. I suddenly saw a fresh purpose in my interactions with others. Was someone discouraged? I could comfort. Was someone weary? I would refresh them with my words.

As I studied the Bible that summer, I knew that encouragement wasn't only reserved for those with a special gift; we're told repeatedly in Scripture to encourage those around us. For example, in 2 Corinthians 13:11, Paul gives us a goal for which to aim: "Finally, brothers and sisters, rejoice! Strive for full restoration, encourage one another, be of one mind, live in peace. And the God of love and peace will be with you" (NIV). Paul also tells us to "encourage one another and build each other up" (1 Thess. 5:11 NIV) and, in fact, to "encourage one another daily" as a regular habit (Heb. 3:13 NIV). I also loved considering how God promises something special for those who encourage others; a wise proverb states, "Whoever refreshes others will be refreshed" (Prov. 11:25 NIV).

> **What if we began to see our conversations as a way to refresh others in the Lord and to encourage them?**

What if we began to see our conversations as a way to refresh others in the Lord and to encourage them? Paul himself confesses in a letter to Philemon that he needed refreshment. He asks his friend to "refresh [his] heart in Christ" (v. 20). A great model for conversation stems from this need for mutual refreshment. We read in Romans 1:11–12 Paul's desire that might mirror our own. He writes, "I long to see you so that I may impart to you some spiritual gift to make you strong—that is, that you and I may be *mutually encouraged* by each other's faith" (NIV). Paul reminds in Ephesians 4:29 to "not let any unwholesome talk come out of your mouths, but only what is helpful for building others up according to their needs" (NIV). What if we entered every conversation by first imagining what would help build others up? How different our interactions could become both in person and virtually if we adopted this goal to aid interpersonal closeness!

But how? What does it mean to refresh another person? What kinds of words bring encouragement to others? If you look throughout Scripture at times when people felt most discouraged, you'll find similar themes in how others encouraged them. These themes involve reminding people of God's presence, His work on their behalf, and His unique gifting of them. Moses (Deut. 31:8), Joshua (Josh.1:9), David (1 Chron. 28:20) and, most notably, Jesus (Matt. 28:20) all encouraged discouraged people with the truth that God will never leave them or forsake them. Perhaps the most comforting encouragement comes from Psalm 46:1 that "God is our refuge and strength, an ever-present help in trouble" (NIV). ***Reminding others of God's presence that won't leave or forsake them matters deeply in times of discouragement.***

Likewise, when talking to struggling people, we can remind them of a profound truth first noted in 2 Chronicles 20:15 that the "battle is not [ours], but God's." I recently attended a prayer meeting where the leader asked us all to name a burden we were carrying in our lives. We were to tell the Lord something like, "Lord, I have been carrying this burden, and now I hand it over to You to take care of for me." People stated their burdens with health, children, and work—anything troubling their hearts—and experienced the great refreshment and encouragement to let God "daily bears our burdens" (Ps. 68:19 NIV). *Reminding others that God can carry their burdens offers encouragement in overwhelming times.*

Finally, when speaking in conversation, we might also point out spiritual gifts, strengths, and progress we see. We see the writers of the New Testament letters offering encouraging words for what they see in their readers. Paul tells the readers of 1 Corinthians how enriched they have become in knowledge and how they have many spiritual gifts (1 Cor.1:4–7). In Colossians 1:3–5, Paul points out the faith and love of the readers and how thankful he is for them. In 1 Thessalonians 1:2–10, Paul compliments the hard work and perseverance of the Christ followers there. *Reminding others of their good character, unique gifts, or hard work offers great encouragement to those who need personal encouragement.*

If you are reading this as someone from a different spiritual tradition, or if you aren't comfortable talking in these ways, you can still offer encouragement in broader ways that *you* are with them and that *you* are caring for them.

3 WAYS TO OFFER ENCOURAGEMENT AND REFRESHMENT TO OTHERS

1. Remind them they are not alone; you are with them and so is the Holy Spirit.

    Things to say: *God is with you. He's not against you. He won't leave you. You are not alone. I'm not going anywhere either. You can talk to me.*

2. Refocus their heart on God's care for them. If they are not Christians or religious in any way, you can ask if you can pray for them.

Things to say: *Let's ask God to help us. You don't have to carry this burden. What do we need to ask God for right now?*

3. Compliment their strengths, acts of service, and spiritual gifts.

Things to say: *I noticed you are a truly excellent _____. You seem to have a special gift for _____. I love how you always_____. Thank you for how you_____.*

PERSONAL INVENTORY

1. When I enter a conversation, I like to remind people that God is near.

Never　　　　　**Sometimes**　　　　　**Usually**

Try memorizing a passage of Scripture about the nearness of God (Deut. 31:6; Phil. 4:5; Ps. 46:1) and reminding a family member or friend about God's "ever-present help."

2. When I enter a conversation, I can figure out how to direct the conversation toward prayer to help others "cast their anxieties" on the Lord (1 Peter 5:7).

Never　　　　　**Sometimes**　　　　　**Usually**

Try asking others (even people who are not yet Christians) this question: If you could summarize what's going on in terms of one thing you'd ask me to pray for you regarding this discouraging situation, what should we pray?

3. When I enter a conversation, I think about how to compliment others to encourage them.

Never   **Sometimes**   **Usually**

Try offering a compliment to each person in your family today. Then try to encourage friends and coworkers by noticing something they said or did that blessed you.

Close Conversations for Personal Growth
But if you aim to learn or achieve something with others, friendship happens naturally during the shared pursuit.—James Clear

In addition to serving as a college professor, I also work as a consultant to help others achieve their writing goals, so naturally, I love helping others get to their next step in life. In fact, my favorite kinds of conversations—and the ones that make me feel deeply connected to others—involve our mutual sharing of professional goals, life dreams, creative endeavors, and long-term plans.

Every month, my husband and I join great friends for a dinner out to have conversations about personal growth. We share what we're learning and need to learn, what we're working toward professionally and personally, and our dreams for the future. During this dinner, we ask questions of one another designed to "spur one another on toward love and good deeds" (Heb. 10:24 NIV). These questions might follow the design of the Six Conversations, where we ask about growth in the social, emotional, physical, cognitive, volitional, and spiritual areas. While we eat burgers and fries at our favorite local restaurant, we offer wisdom and insight to one another; we connect ideas together in ways that catalyze action; we brainstorm ways around obstacles to

> *Think about your favorite people to talk to in your life. Notice how they inspire you to achieve your goals and how they express concern about your life.*

our dreams. We also use the time to widen our circle of friendship to include others who also care about the same personal or professional goals.

These friendships are so joyful and make us feel so meaningfully connected that I've learned to think about *every* conversation as a way to help others grow in any area. As a Christian especially, I think about helping others become excited to know Jesus better after spending time with me. I remember how Paul wrote that he would "remain and continue [with his friends in Philippi], for [their] progress and joy in the faith" (Phil. 1:24–25). I love how Paul describes his friend Timothy as another friend who would be "genuinely concerned for [their] welfare" because everyone else just "[seeks] their own interests" (Phil. 2:20–21a). What if you saw your presence in conversation as a way to help others grow and to demonstrate genuine concern for how they were doing? Also think about your favorite people to talk to in your life. Notice how they inspire you to achieve your goals and how they express concern about your life. Notice how they ask good questions to support you in your dreams. What if you were that person to someone today? What if everyone became that person to someone else?

3 WAYS TO SEE CONVERSATION AS HELPING EACH OTHER GROW

1. Ask others about their professional or personal goals, creative projects, or long-term dreams in conversation. You might ask easy questions like these:

   What projects have you been working on lately?
   Where have you felt stuck lately in your goals in life?

Have you been working on any creative projects?
What's next for you?

2. Think about how you can offer support by asking others how *they like to be supported in their goals.* Some friends like to celebrate milestones; others like for you to check in on their progress as a form of accountability.

3. As you think about the Six Conversations, you can move through a series of questions based on the six dimensions of being human to help people enjoy progress. Ask these questions:

Who can I connect you with to help you with this? (social)

How are you feeling emotionally about where you are right now? (emotional)

Do you have any physical limitations preventing you from this goal? (physical)

What's your strategy moving forward, and how can I help? (cognitive)

What choices do you have in the next week related to this goal? (volitional)

What can we ask God for regarding your next steps? (spiritual)

PERSONAL INVENTORY

1. When I enter a conversation, I like to ask people about their personal goals, current projects, or long-term dreams. I also like to share these things with others.

Never   **Sometimes**   **Usually**

Try writing down a list of current short-term and long-term goals, current projects (either personal or professional), and dreams you'd like to one day see come true. What if you started a conversation by talking about a current project and then asking your friend what project he or she is working on?

2. When I enter a conversation, I can figure out how to help people think about their next best step to grow personally.

Never   **Sometimes**   **Usually**

Try asking others what they think their next best step is to achieve their goals or grow personally. Then, offer encouragement about what you see might help them achieve their goals.

3. When I enter a conversation, I think about how to collaborate with others to grow together professionally or personally.

Never   **Sometimes**   **Usually**

Try looking for ways to work with other people on your projects or personal goals. Who in your life might serve as a practical source of help, inspiration, or encouragement for mutual growth? Reach out to this person and see how you might also become involved in the goals and dreams they care about.

Close Conversations through Marveling

Imagine a great conversation you're having. You're encouraging one another. You're asking about dreams and goals and helping one another think about your progress in any area. Is that all? Is there another secret to connection and to feeling close to one another? Is there something so wonderful that we cannot believe we haven't attempted to incorporate it in our daily interactions with others?

This missing element in conversational closeness involves a beautiful concept: *awe*. In my literature research at both the University of Virginia and the University of Michigan, I centered my inquiries of literature around the notion of awe and, more specifically, sublime experiences. Awe involves marveling at something sacred, vast, supernatural, mysterious, and so beautiful you feel overcome by the thing you're thinking about or experiencing, eighteenth-century philosopher Edmund Burke observed.[1] More recently, psychologists identify awe as a powerful emotional state of "wonderment and mystery . . . and moving people toward a feeling of being more interconnected."[2] In a research study in which psychologists interviewed participants on their experience of awe, they identified key themes: "connection with the universe, connection with the divine, and connection with all living things." The researchers discussed how the experience of awe brings "people in touch with elements of being that are not typically considered in routine daily activities" which allows for personal growth and awareness of meaning.[3]

What if our conversations helped one another increase our capacity of awe? As I read about the benefits of awe (including how cultivating awe leads to kindness, patience, gratitude, happiness, increasing life satisfaction, creativity, and even lowered inflammation in the body),[4] I decided to take seriously the task of helping others experience awe. I liked what I studied about how awe "reduces self-focus, promotes social connection, and fosters prosocial actions by encouraging a 'small self.'"[5] Researchers, for example, state this about awe:

> In addition to shaping the subjective experience of individuals, awe also has powerful effects on social relationships. Feelings of awe help us to put our problems into perspective and to prioritize the needs of the collective above our own. By shifting attention

away from the self and onto the outside world, awe diminishes feelings of self-importance and makes people feel smaller, yet more connected, to a larger community and purpose.[6]

In particular, I wanted to see in action the research that awe makes people feel more *social and more connected* to each other.[7] Would it put our problems in perspective? Would people connect more?

First, I had to think carefully about how to promote awe in my conversational patterns. How do we foster the unique well-being generated by awe-inducing conversation? If I asked students what makes them full of "awe" in their research or classes, what would happen?

I shared this research with my students and challenged them to cultivate sustained curiosity that leads to awe in their careers. "Awe," I told them, "staves off boredom. It keeps you creative, happy, and connected both to ideas and to people."

I put on some music and asked the class to write for five minutes about what in their current research fascinates them to the point of awe. Where do they tap into mystery? What feels so weird or unknown that it's like they've connected to the supernatural? "Think about what you cannot explain. Think about that feeling that something amazing is going on."

When I asked students to share what they wrote, the results astounded me. Normally reticent students pumped their hands into the air for me to call on them. As each student shared what deeply fascinates them to the point of awe, other students began asking them questions. People began connecting over shared awe. If the concepts sounded too technical, students kept asking questions. That day, I learned about folding mirrors in space, about quantum gravity, and about neuromorphic computing. In this advanced technical writing course of engineers and STEM majors, I had students connecting deeply over topics as varied as cloud storage and injury reduction in gymnastics. And they kept talking. And they talked about their futures together. One student who wants to earn a PhD as she studies black holes mentioned collaborating in the future with a physics student who couldn't stop talking about imaginary numbers and the square roots of negative numbers alongside his passion for quantum physics.

And me? The grammar expert? I had no idea what anyone was talking about, but I felt connected just being there and sharing everyone's joy. My contribution to the conversation included this statement: "When you write about quantum gravity and neuromorphic computing, use strong verbs. Use a colon. Move your verbs to the front of your sentence!"

"Of course!" one student said, beaming. "We would *never* forget the strong verb!"

Every walk with my friend and mentor, Sandy, becomes an "awe walk." I learned about "awe walks" through an interesting research study from 2020.[8] Psychologists from the University of California and San Francisco State wanted to provide an intervention for the aging population because of their concern that "aging into later life is often accompanied by social disconnection, anxiety, and sadness." Especially concerning to the researchers involves the data that decreased social connection can "hasten cognitive impairment, physical decline, and even death."[9] Could the experience of awe help build social connection, reduce stress, and foster joy? The researchers explain the study:

> Awe—a positive emotion elicited when in the presence of vast things not immediately understood—reduces self-focus, promotes social connection, and fosters prosocial actions by encouraging a "small self." We investigated the emotional benefits of a novel "awe walk" intervention in healthy older adults. Sixty participants took weekly 15-min outdoor walks for 8 weeks; participants

were randomly assigned to an awe walk group, which oriented them to experience awe during their walks . . ."[10]

For their experience on the "awe walk," participants were instructed to "experience awe by tapping into their sense of wonder and walking in new locales."[11]

As we walk through our neighborhood together, Sandy stops to point out something like beautiful flowers. She'll actually stand before blooming lavender and sing praises to God with her hands lifted up to heaven. Sandy lives an awe-filled life, and she's teaching me to do the same through the questions she asks me. "Do you see that bird? Did you ever consider that God didn't have to make birds? And He didn't have to make them *sing*, either." We walk on, marveling as we hear the cry of a hawk or the melody of a chirping sparrow. When Sandy talks to me, my problems suddenly feel smaller. My heart grows for worship. I feel the awe inside of me as we notice the blue hydrangea. I feel close to God and to Sandy.

My younger daughter and I began taking a daily walk during the isolation of the COVID-19 pandemic. We didn't call it an awe walk (we called it "taking loops"), but that's what our walk became. First, we marveled over icicles and snowfall until we stood in awe over crocuses peeking through the black earth. We talked about the rabbits and the deer that spilled into our neighborhood from the woods behind our home. We noticed the changing seasons. We asked questions about acorns and pumpkins and hooting owls in the dusky tree limbs. One day, we caught sight of the International Space Station whizzing past overhead and called out "Hello! Hello, up there!"—in awe that by the time we checked our phones to see the actual position of the space station, it had already passed Brazil.

The best part of my walks with Sandy and my daughter involves that moment when we feel smaller because Something Else feels big. We catch wind of divine activity in nature and also in our own lives.

We talk about God's work in our ordinary days, how He's answering prayer, and the mystery that we can feel His presence. These walks during that time—in the midst of so much suffering all around—helped us feel interconnected to one another, to our larger community, and to God. It's how we survived.

Speaking Words of Worship

In the Bible, we observe a new way of talking to one another that connects us to divine activity. Instead of the lower forms of discourse—what Paul asks us to put away from our lives (including anger, malice, slander, and obscenity)—we're invited to "let the word of Christ dwell in [us] richly, teaching and admonishing one another in all wisdom, singing psalms and hymns and spiritual songs, with thankfulness in [our] hearts to God" (Col. 3:16–17). I think of Sandy singing a hymn of praise about the flowers and urging me to grow in thankfulness. I think of wise people I know who always seem to quote a timely Bible verse or encourage me.

In college, I used foul language and mostly complained and gossiped about others. As I read both Colossians and Ephesians, I wondered if I could ever become the kind of person who spoke in "psalms, hymns, and songs from the Spirit" (Eph. 5:19 NIV). Could I truly "make music in my heart to the Lord" and share that with others in conversation? David urges in Psalm 40 not to hide these conversations. Instead, David writes, "I speak of your faithfulness and your saving help. I do not conceal your love and faithfulness from the great assembly" (v. 10 NIV). When I read those words from David, I thought about the "assemblies" in my life: my roommates, classmates and professors, students, and neighbors. What if I began speaking about God to lead people to awe? What if my personal mission became to *help others marvel*?

3 WAYS TO HELP OTHERS MARVEL IN CONVERSATION

1. Ask others when they last experienced awe. Where were they? What was happening? What did it feel like? Who was there? What happened next?
2. Actively observe what's happening around you. You can ask, "Did you notice that? Isn't that mysterious or curious?"
3. Ask questions about what people are celebrating and what they are thankful for. These conversations lead to gratitude which often leads to worship.

PERSONAL INVENTORY

1. I regularly experience awe in my life. I know what this feels like and how to talk about it.

Never　　　　　　**Sometimes**　　　　　　**Usually**

Try cultivating a sense of awe by recording answers to prayer (divine activity), examining nature, or thinking about things in your life that create a sense of mystery, beauty, or wonder. Take an "awe walk" and record what you experienced. For more helpful tips, consider the article "7 Ways to Be Awe-Inspired in Everyday Life." The author, psychology professor Andy Tix, encourages readers to take an awe walk to encounter something vast in nature. He writes:

> Identify some ways you might personally connect with something vast in nature that stretches your perspective. Maybe you could sit by a large open area of natural beauty, such as a nearby vista, lake, or river. Perhaps you could behold a local stand of towering trees or the intricate details of flowers around your home. If there is a particular wild animal that

lives near you that causes you to stop in your tracks, you could identify when they are most likely to be observed in their natural habitat and go there at that time. A starry night, the northern lights, the rising or setting sun, and the unfolding of a storm all provide opportunities to be awestruck. If you've had multiple encounters with the same source of awe, look for new ways to be astonished.[12]

Tix also encourages building an "awe portfolio" in a journal or in a photo album to remember your experiences of feeling awe.[13]

2. When I enter a conversation, I like to talk about things that make me marvel or create a sense of wonder. I can tell others the things I think about when I worship.

Never   **Sometimes**   **Usually**

3. When I enter a conversation, I think about how, by the end of our interaction, I can help people thank God and have an attitude of praise.

Never   **Sometimes**   **Usually**

Try noticing what seems like divine activity in the lives of those around you (provision, answered prayer, providential circumstances) and tell your friend what you perceive. Practice telling others when you notice something God is doing in your life.

When I think about adding value to people's lives and blessing them in conversation—and how to build the warm connections so vital for our well-being—I remember these Three Fresh Goals of a good conversation, and I allow these goals to shape my questions, my commentary, and how I share about my life. I can ponder before I speak these questions:

Will this question, comment, or personal story help *encourage* this person?

Will this question, comment, or personal story help us *grow and work toward our goals*?

Will this question, comment, or personal story help us *reach a state of marveling, awe, or worship*? In other words, am I speaking in a way that adds to human flourishing by urging others toward hope and joy?

When I think about the Three Fresh Goals of Conversation, I feel inspired to live and speak in new ways. These goals provide a focus and a plan for what I wish to happen in even my most ordinary conversations. These goals challenge me to discover why I'm not having these kinds of conversations and what pitfalls I continually fall into as I try to warmly connect with others. The next chapter reveals these pitfalls and helps us avoid them on our journey to loving conversations.

CHAPTER FIVE

WHAT GOES WRONG IN CONVERSATION

Do all things without grumbling or disputing, that you may be blameless and innocent, children of God without blemish in the midst of a crooked and twisted generation, among whom you shine as lights in the world.

—Philippians 2:14–15

THE FOUR MINDSETS of a Loving Conversation and the Three Fresh Goals of Conversations create conversational closeness, warmth, and purposeful connections. But, on the flipside, we can harm, disrupt, and even sabotage our conversations. As I set out to study the literature regarding toxic conversational behaviors, as well as gathering the opinions of others, I discovered ten poor conversational attitudes and behaviors—what I call the Ten Pitfalls to Avoid in Conversation. We can analyze our own conversations first, and then consider the strategies to avoid these pitfalls:

Criticizing

Complaining

Advice-giving

Self-absorption

Divisiveness

Flattery

Manipulation

Codependence

Gossip

Arrogance

EXAMINING OUR CONVERSATIONAL GOALS

As we think about developing satisfying and warm relationships—and the wonderful purpose of meaningful conversations to connect, encourage others, share our lives, and love people well—is a great time to ask *what's going wrong* in our conversational patterns. Self-examination in this area leads to significant improvement in our friendships as we honestly assess toxic patterns in how we relate to others.

I know what you're thinking. It's *other* people who make it hard for you to have close relationships. They are the problem, right? Not me! While you might use the list above to notice and ultimately redirect your friends who engage in the listed behaviors, first start with yourself. As you think through this list, it's not a time to feel judged or condemned. It's a time to grow and ask God to help you become more like Jesus. It's a time to consider how the ten behaviors and attitudes below poison conversation and hinder warm, loving connections.

Then? We start fresh with new, healthy conversations.

As I've studied the research literature on relational closeness and talked to hundreds of students about what they most respect in other people, I compiled the above list to help us become the joyful, godly, and wise conversation partners that enact the Three Fresh Goals of

Conversation. What then, in our conversational patterns *hinders encouragement, personal growth, and marveling*? What do we do in conversation that discourages, thwarts growth, and prevents feelings of awe? In that above list, you'll find how each pitfall works to harm the Three Fresh Goals.

Discouragement

Let's start with discouragement. In conversation, if we adopt a posture of *complaining, criticism,* or *constant advice-giving,* we set a tone that prevents joyful, loving connection. When we encourage others in conversations, we're rejoicing with them (or mourning if they need it). We're looking for the good. We're helping to point out what's going well. The positive mood associated with thanksgiving and complimenting—or anything you do to create a good mood—helps others problem-solve, become more creative, focus their attention, and even learn better.[1] With the science of education and the role of positive mood for classroom success, I take seriously the choices I made to create good feelings in my classroom. The same applies to conversation. Biblically, I also enact in conversation Paul's command to "do everything without grumbling or complaining" (Phil. 2:14 NIV) and to "give thanks in all circumstances" (1 Thess. 5:18).

I remember the summer I stopped complaining about *everything*. I worked at Camp Greystone—a Christian summer camp that deeply valued a form of positive thinking that, at first, I thought was surely unbiblical. Why were the directors and staff always so cheerful? Why did they demonstrate thankful hearts and find the good in everything? How could anyone be so positive *all the time*? After six summers of working at Greystone, I learned what happens to a heart that trusts in God's sovereignty, goodness, and ability to "work all things for good." I learned to speak to others in a way that highlighted what was going right—not always what was going wrong. Suddenly, people wanted to hang out with me. I had more friends than ever before. In fact, people would say, "I need a shot of encouragement from Heather" like I was a vaccine against creeping despair. I also confessed what I learned some Christians called a "critical spirit." Instead of walking into a conversation to talk about everything wrong, I first addressed everything going well. Instead of complaining about something, I would work to fix a problem. Instead of criticizing others, I would speak directly to someone if I needed help understanding their decisions.

Finally, I learned to empower others in conversation rather than always giving advice. I learned to ask, "What do you think you should do? What are your choices? How can I support you?" I learned to wait until someone asked me expressly for my opinion or advice before speaking about what I would do in any situation. To this very day, if someone shares a personal problem, I might say, "Do you want advice? Or do you like it when I ask questions to help you think of different options?" Guess what? Everyone likes the questions. They want to feel smart. They want to feel empowered. Advice-giving diminishes loving connection because it positions you as a counselor or parent rather than a friend. I've known certain people who, when they called or stopped by, I dreaded the interaction because every conversation was about how to improve me, how to solve my problems, or how they would do something differently or better.

Thwarting Personal Growth

What about conversational attitudes and behavior that don't help people grow or achieve their goals? I think of five behaviors or attitudes that, in conversation, don't move people to think about larger goals, dreams, or a fresh vision for their lives—all joyful and loving conversational aims. *Self-absorption* (that manifests as monologuing, only talking about yourself, and not actively listening), *divisiveness* (using conversation to simply stir up controversy and embroil your listener in conflict), *flattery* (empty compliments to try to get your conversation partner to like you), *manipulation* (conversing to gain personal advantage), and *codependence* (excessive reliance on others to solve problems for either person). Instead, loving conversations that help others grow involve focusing on others, building unity, affirming others in a genuine way, enjoying the conversation to build connections instead of using a person for your advantage, and empowering people to grow in interdependence and not in codependence with others. Empowering people to solve their own problems and assuming responsibility for their emotional well-being helps them grow and aids their progress to emotional maturity. Your role in a loving conversation is supportive connection where you listen and think about ways to help others develop their gifts and talents.

Sabotaging Awe

Finally, if one of the goals of a loving, joyful, and connected conversation involves experiencing awe, what prevents our journey toward marveling, fascination, mystery, and even worship? I think of a quote often attributed to Eleanor Roosevelt (though it appeared in newspapers before her lifetime), that "great minds discuss ideas; average minds discuss events; small minds discuss people."[2]

Small minds discuss people. I think of my own tendency to *gossip* and the impact that has on conversation. Sure, it might feel fun to gossip and share juicy morsels of information about others, but does that kind of conversation fill our hearts with awe and wonder as we discuss grand ideas? Can I do better? Instead of gossiping about anyone, I can celebrate others in conversation but then move quickly on to *ideas*. Even asking a friend in the cognitive realm of conversation (one of the Six Conversations) about what they're thinking about or what new ideas they've had recently will immediately shift the conversation to the realm of ideas.

But something else prevents arriving to awe in a conversation: *arrogance*. It might be hard to admit to yourself, but how often do you feel *superior* to others? How often do you feel like others have nothing to offer you because, perhaps, of their education, socioeconomic status, ethnicity, background, or gender? In an article simply entitled "Arrogance," in *American Philosophical Quarterly* back in 1998, we find a perfect description of an arrogant person as it relates to conversation:

> His perceived status as a more excellent human being shapes his relations with others. Since he is superior to others, he does not regard others as having anything to offer him, nor does he believe they have the ability to enrich his life. The views and opinions of others are not of interest to him, and he treats them with disdain. Others owe him, in virtue of his excellence, a special sort of deference. He therefore establishes hierarchical and nonreciprocal relationships with his fellow human beings. These relationships are marked by a lack of the mutual enrichment that is ... an essential component of true friendship.[3]

An arrogant person fails to form warm connections because he or she fails in the Four Mindsets of a Loving Conversation; they don't believe the best about others and they refuse interpersonal curiosity, investing, and mutual sharing. An arrogant person doesn't care about what other people think at all.

In contrast, a humble person believes every person offers something of value. Every person they encounter might teach them something, grant them a fresh perspective, or support and help them in just the way they need. A humble person positions themselves to experience awe because of what they experience by being with another person.

Consider again the ten pitfalls to avoid in conversation. Mark the categories you most struggle with. I personally marked criticizing others, gossiping, flattering, or manipulating others as danger areas for me because I can often fall into these patterns. What about you?

10 PITFALLS IN CONVERSATION INVENTORY

Criticizing

It's easy for me to find what's wrong about a situation or a person. I enjoy pointing out what isn't working or what I don't like about something. Most of my conversations involve me telling others what offends me or upsets me about someone.

Complaining

It's natural for me to complain about how bad my day is going. I complain about my work, my problems, my health, and my family. I have a difficult time expressing gratitude or finding out what's going well.

Advice-giving

When people share a problem with me, I immediately tell them what to do because I have experienced that and have wisdom. I always know what's best for people.

Self-absorption

I love to talk about myself and focus on what I need. When I'm in conversation, I cannot wait for you to stop talking so I can share my ideas and what I need from you. I often speak for long stretches and expect others to listen attentively.

Divisiveness

I often pit people against each other or speak in a way that's "us versus them." I believe we have real enemies, and it's my job to warn you about how bad other people are. I'm not interested in finding common ground with people who believe differently from me about religion or politics.

Flattery

I want people to like me, so I find ways to compliment them even if I don't believe what I'm saying. I want people to feel good around me, so I say disingenuous things. I just want to please people.

Manipulation

In conversation, I like to think about what I can get from a person or how I can use them to my advantage to advance my goals. I believe strongly in networking and in finding friends who have power or prestige so they can help me in my goals. I also speak to people to secretly get them to do what I want.

Codependence

I like people needing me and wanting me to solve their problems. I want my children, spouse, friends, and coworkers to always need me. I also expect others to always be there for me to make me feel better and solve my problems. I'm always checking in on my friends and feel anxious if too many hours go by without me knowing how they are doing.

Gossip

Most of my conversations involve sharing private information about others, talking about the lives of other people, or asking about other people's misfortunes so I can feel better about myself.

Arrogance

I often believe I am better than others because of my financial status, ethnicity, race, education, or gender. I am bored by the interests and opinions of others and would rather talk about my own ideas. I see myself as superior to others and do not think they have anything of real value to offer me.

As you look at the above questions, think carefully about changes you want to make in your conversational patterns.

Sometimes when I share this list, people immediately categorize their friends and know what bothers them in conversation. I learned in a professional development seminar a beautiful way to help guide others out of the pitfalls. You can say things like this:

"Hey! I experience you as complaining all the time. I didn't know if you meant to come off this way." I said this to a friend, and she immediately said, "Oh my goodness, really? Really? I'm so sorry! I guess I am a downer. I didn't realize that everyone thought that about me. I just don't know what to do except complain." You can substitute another pitfall in for complaining.

"Hey! I noticed that we're gossiping a lot, and I want to work on that personally. Would you mind if our conversations didn't involve gossip anymore?" My friend said that to me ten years ago, and I loved her for it.

While this may have been a difficult chapter to read, I hope it has inspired you as it inspired me. We can think this right now for our next conversation: Instead of our old patterns in conversation, we can use this next conversation to encourage, help another person achieve their goals, and foster in us both a state of awe. Imagine your next conversation ending with your friend saying to you, "I feel so encouraged. Thank you. I'm excited for what's next for me. I feel closer to God and full of wonder after talking to you. What a beautiful conversation that was!"

PART TWO

Fresh
Conversations

CHAPTER SIX

REVISITING THE BASICS

Everyone is interesting, but it's not up to them to show you—it's up to you to discover it.

—Georgie Nightingall, conversation expert

THIS PAST YEAR, I'VE revisited the basics of how to serve as a great conversation partner. It's a lifelong skill we might continue to hone—no matter how old we are, smart we are, or extroverted we feel. Everyone needs help when it comes to loving others better in conversations. As a community building and growing conversation expert who regularly spends time with people who seek development as conversationalists, I discovered an easy way to remember the basics of how to have a good conversation: four categories that all begin with the letter "L" for better recall. You are practicing good conversational skills if you are:

Letting others speak

Listening

Limiting distractions

Loving through your face

These categories may seem obvious or intuitive, but I share my best and often-overlooked tips for better conversation. Once you've practiced these skills, we can then think about how to ask the first questions, move into follow-up questions, and how to keep a conversation going. My students love this training, especially for awkward first conversations like first dates, sorority or fraternity rushing, dinner interviews, new group assignments in class, and for the start of their clubs on campus.

PRACTICE GOOD CONVERSATION SKILLS

Letting Others Speak

When you enter a new conversation, think first about the goal of letting others speak. This matters because sometimes we position ourselves as needing to share our opinions and thoughts on a topic. We aim to talk rather than considering the two-way goal of a better conversation. I'm a reformed monologue-giver and interrupter. I'm someone who loved to spout all my opinions and talk and talk and talk. And if you were talking, believe me, I'd interrupt you with my own feelings or personal stories to turn the conversation back to me. Nobody wants or needs a friend like this. But how did I change?

I learned the art of *conversational turn-taking* and practiced not speaking for more than a few minutes at a time.

Try it. Set a timer if you must for no more than two minutes. If the goal of a loving conversation is warm connection, you might now wonder what to do after your two minutes of talking. Well, you pause. You see if the other person has something to say. When you pause, the other person has time to ask a meaningful question, make an observation, or connect to their own experience. In that pause, you might also ask your conversation partner one of the categories of the Six Conversations. Say, for example, your friend has asked about your day. You share about something you've accomplished at work or something you're struggling with. After two minutes or less, you can pause. Then you can move in this direction of conversation:

Have you felt this way? What did you do? (emotional and volitional)
What about you? How did you feel about your day? (emotional)
Did you see anyone interesting? (social)
Did you feel good physically all day? How did you sleep? (physical)
Did you have to make any hard choices today? (volitional)
Did you learn anything cool today? (cognitive)
What did you think about during that meeting? (cognitive)
Did you feel especially close to God today? (spiritual)

Essentially, conversational turn-taking involves the volley of questions and answers, of sharing longer stories when necessary and thinking of conversation as a warm connection. It's not therapy or a one-sided monologue. It's *connection.*

Tip: Set your phone timer to 2 minutes when you start talking to a friend. See how long that actually feels.

If you monologue or interrupt like me, I can tell you there's hope. If there's hope for someone like me, there's hope for someone like you. I have a few friends who monologue. They know they struggle with talking too much, so I've shared with them the two-minute strategy of conversational turn-taking. I've also shared how to avoid *interrupting* others. When my daughter was little, her sister continually interrupted her. She would cry out, "Mom, she broke my voice!" Sarah wasn't too far off in her description of interrupting; etymologically, it derives from the Latin word "to break." When you speak over people or interrupt them, it's a way of breaking their thought and harming the conversation.

> *Loving conversationalists limit interrupting. They wait. They're patient. They let others talk. Instead of interrupting, they become better listeners.*

Now, I'm part Italian, and I live in a northern state. Many of my closest friends are from New York or New Jersey. We're fast-talkers. We're interrupters. We're loud and domineering in conversation with our hands flying everywhere and our opinions ricocheting off the walls. It's funny to witness, but sometimes, it harms people who can't find their way into a conversation. Once, at an Italian dinner party, the youngest daughter at the table approached her father with tears in her eyes. He leaned down to her, and I heard her whimper, "Daddy, I cannot find my space to talk." Her big Italian father with his booming voice raised his hand to silence the table and said, "This one has something to say."

I think about that little girl who couldn't find her space in conversation. I'm learning that loving conversationalists limit interrupting. They wait. They're patient. They let others talk. Instead of interrupting, *they become better listeners.* Think of a conversation like a space to fill. Let others take up space too.

Listening

I'm most growing in the area of listening well. I used to believe listening simply meant paying attention and hearing what my conversation partner said. But no! This year I learned *what to listen for.* This became a life-changing moment of transformation for me when I realized how to listen. What should you listen *for* as someone talks to you?

LISTEN FOR TRANSFORMATION. LISTEN FOR THE STORY OF CHANGE.
I recently sat at a lunch table with five complete strangers at a speaking event. Nobody spoke. Nobody asked me one question, and nobody

asked each other even one question. I took a deep breath because I felt exhausted and more introverted than I had ever felt in my life. I just wanted to go home and take a bubble bath and not speak to anyone for the next three days. But instead, I remembered the beauty and joy of loving conversations. I remembered that these strangers might have something to teach me and some wisdom to share. So I began asking questions about their lives. I threw out so many questions (Do you garden? Do you like to cook? How long have you lived here? Do you have children?). Guess what? I received one-word answers. Crickets after that. Ugh! Here I sat, a conversation expert, and I couldn't figure out any way to get this table connected. I asked God to help me.

Then, I remembered how to ask questions and listen for transformation and a story of change. I asked one question that revitalized the course of that quiet lunch and left us all feeling warmly connected. I asked the woman to my right this question: "How long have you been in the consulting business?"

"Only three years. I started my business at fifty years old," she said and speared her salad. She didn't look at me.

"Wow! That's amazing. Fifty years old! What happened at that age to make you start a business?"

Suddenly, her eyes gleamed. She turned to face me, put her fork down, and said, "It took me that long to realize my true passion. I was so bored before, and then one day . . ."

The table leaned in. We were hooked on the story of transformation of how a woman took the bold risk to form her own company and why. After she shared her story, I realized her core value of risk-taking and adventure. I wondered if I could ever be that courageous in my own career. I turned to strangers who now began to feel like friends when I asked, "Have any of you ever done something you would describe as professionally courageous?"

That's all it took. We sat together, mutually inspired and connected.

We laughed together as we decided as a group to eat our dessert before the main course—as our first courageous act to go against the norm. That day, I no longer felt homesick or lonely or bored. I didn't want to go home to my bubble bath. I wanted to spend more time talking about courage and our professional lives. Weeks later, I thought of those new friends who laughed and ate dessert too soon and who would think for the first time about taking a fresh risk in their own lives. On my drive home, I wondered what my next "professionally courageous act" could be. Maybe it's writing this book.

As we listen for stories of transformation in our new friends, we might also consider the words of community building expert Margaret Wheatley who wrote a life-changing phrase in her book *Turning to One Another: Simple Conversations to Restore Hope to the Future.* She writes that, in great conversations, we need to take a particular posture of what she calls the "willingness to be disturbed."[1] When we listen to others, we might listen for what unsettles us, surprises us, or challenges us. And then, instead of reacting, we might ask questions using the Four Mindsets of curiosity, positive regard, investment, and mutual sharing. When my conversation partner told me about her new consulting busines—launched at age fifty—I did feel surprised and unsettled. Her risk-taking challenged my ideas of a stable career, but I knew I could learn from her. I found myself invested in her success, so I asked about how many clients she had and what projects they work on together. I then shared about my own new opportunities and wondered about how she overcame fear and insecurity. By the end, I realized as I listened *for what surprised me* and felt different about this woman, I could connect more deeply with her and even with myself. Wheatley writes: "Listen as best you can for what's different, for what surprises you. See if this practice helps you learn something new. Notice whether you develop a better relationship with the person you're talking with. If you try this with several people, you might find yourself laughing in delight as you realize how many unique ways there are to be human."[2]

LISTEN FOR THE STORY OF CHANGE OR TRANSFORMATION.
LISTEN FOR WHAT SURPRISES YOU, UNSETTLES YOU,
OR DISTURBS YOU. LISTEN TO SUPPORT.

Besides learning to listen for what surprises or unsettles me as someone speaks, I'm learning to position myself as a supportive listener. As I researched this idea of "supportive listening," I learned what a profound act of love it is to truly listen to someone with our full attention. Researchers publishing in the *International Journal of Listening* state,

> When we listen to others, we offer not only our time but also our psychological presence, our cognitive attention, and our emotional responsiveness, all of which are finite and thus valuable interpersonal resources. Extending the effort to listen to someone may therefore be conceptualized as an expression of affection for that person, at least in situations when listening is not otherwise expected or compensated.[3]

Think of supportive listening as offering your full self—everything you are—in that moment.

Once you've given your full presence in conversation, now what? Well, this part truly excites me because it's a skill we fail to learn or teach well. Supportive listening involves *listening for a whole narrative and interpreting the information someone gives you to make a larger story about their lives*. Researchers call this "synthesizing conversational information" and actively trying to interpret what people say to assign meaning to it.[4] How does this look practically? What are we actually listening for? We are listening for themes, repeating ideas, and most importantly, core values. We are listening for how to help others make sense of what's happening to them and place it into the larger story of what we know about them.

As I tried to figure out how to become a supportive listener, I was randomly reading a leadership book on how to bring out the best in those I was leading at Penn State. In his book *Extraordinary Influence: How Great Leaders Bring Out the Best in Others*, Dr. Tim Irwin alerts us to how to speak what he calls "words of life" to people.[5] I found myself practically shaking with joy as I learned to listen for a person's core values as they speak so I could then speak life-giving words to them. As I discern those values, I can point them out in conversation and help others feel nurtured and inspired. Irwin lists several core values to observe (integrity, courage, humility, good judgment, authenticity, self-regulation, wisdom, candor, resilience, and influence) to name in others as a way to bring out the best in them. When I thought about the Three Fresh Goals of Conversation (encouragement, progress, and marveling), I thought of Irwin's core values as the missing link I needed in conversation. I'm listening for core values. I'm listening to hear what people truly care about most of all.

I recently aimed to forge a warm connection with a businessperson in our town. Our friendship was growing, but I didn't yet feel that bond of a deeper connection. As we spoke one day, she began talking about a project in which she didn't feel like she was able to do her best work. As I listened, I realized something about her: she deeply valued *excellence* as her top core value. In fact, many of our conversations related to whether or not she felt successful in certain projects. The narrative of her life involves *success*. I commented, "It sounds like your core value is excellence, and you feel best when you're meeting and exceeding the expectation of others."

She beamed. "Yes! That's right. You know me!" she said with a laugh.

I then moved into some options for supportive questions based on the six conversations. Here are some of the questions I knew I could ask:

What does that feel like when you know you've done a mediocre job? How do you handle it? (emotional)

How long have you valued excellence like this? What's the story? (cognitive)

Who do you tend to seek assistance from? Who helps you succeed? (social)

When you're not at your best, does it affect your body—like your appetite or sleep? (physical)

What choice do you have if you're in a setting where your best skills aren't utilized? (volitional)

Is this something I can pray about for you? (spiritual)

That day, we shared our struggles with anxiety and fear of failure. We talked about our shared value of excellence and both the virtues and vices associated with needing to feel "the best" at something. Afterward, my new friend said, "I really, really like talking with you. Please come by my office next week. It's the highlight of my week to spend time with you!"

After that experience, I applied my theory of listening for core values and making supportive statements to a few other relationships in my life. I would say things like, "You definitely value adventure. I feel like your core value in life is to avoid stagnant, boring days."

"Yes! That's right!"

What would you ask next based on the Six Conversations?

How do you know it's an adventure? What counts as adventure to you? (cognitive)

What's your next adventure? What will you choose to do? (volitional)

Can I come to the next adventure? (social)

Why do you think God made you this way? (spiritual)

What does it feel like when you can't find adventure? (emotional)

Why do you think your body craves adventure so much? Is it adrenaline? (physical)

With my friend who likes adventure, I have learned to love how every conversation pushes me toward a more exciting life. I'm learning to say yes when she wants to hike through the woods in the rain or sit on the fifty-yard line in a huge football stadium or bake an elaborate meal together just for the adventure of it.

> *The simple choice to speak to people based on what they value (not what I value) has changed everything about how I connect with people I've just met.*

This friend also seeks out my core values. Anyone who knows me knows I love talking about Jesus most of all. So my friend will always ask what I'm reading in the Bible, what I'm praying for, and how I'm experiencing Jesus that day.

Sometimes, it's hard to know what someone values, or maybe you don't know them well enough to interpret what they're saying through a lens of their life narrative. That's a perfect situation to ask cognitive questions like, "How do you make sense of that?" or "How does this fit into how you think about your core values and life goals?"

People love to feel understood and really seen. After I practiced identifying the core values of others, I began to celebrate with my daughters any time I could identify a core value in them. I would text my daughter at college about her self-regulation, her resilience through COVID-19 as a college student, and her integrity. She would text back loving statements, and our bond grew as I remembered to listen for core values. The simple choice to speak to people based on what *they* value (not what I value) has changed everything about how I parent, how I teach, and how I connect with people I've just met. In fact, in the research on the core principles of close relationships, psychologists note that how close we feel in a relationship depends on whether we feel someone understands what we value—the "extent to which they are cognizant of, sensitive to, and behaviorally supportive of each other's core needs and values."[6]

As the conversation continues, position yourself as a curious learner. Think of how you might grow as a person. After all, a leading researcher in "optimal listening" in conversation claims we need to bring "a kind of presence to other beings in which one is receptive and open to being influenced by them."[7]

Limiting Distractions

While most of us already know the basics of limiting distractions (not looking at your cellphone, focusing on the person speaking, not multitasking), you might not realize that the *mere presence* of a cellphone creates distraction in both conversation partners. Even having the cellphone present on a table during a meal, for example, creates the illusion of distraction and lack of focus.[8] I also personally love when I'm talking to a person and they make a deliberate effort to put away their phone. It feels loving, like they are consciously choosing to focus their attention on me. I recently ran into a student on campus. I called out his name, and he not only turned to face me, but he also took the time to take out his earphones and put his phone in his pocket to give me his full attention. Contrast this with the friend who keeps listening to her Spotify playlist and scrolling through Instagram while you're trying to tell her about concerning bloodwork results. This person's eyes kept darting about to see if she knew anyone passing by, and she actually answered a text *while I was talking to her.* I remembered how that made me feel, so I not only put my phone away, but I put it on silent mode or "Do Not Disturb" when I'm in a conversation with someone.

But there's another dimension to limiting distractions that I've learned in the past decade of creating warm connections with others. If you position yourself as a learner with interpersonal curiosity, you won't just put your phone away. You'll keep a notebook. I'm not talking about a notebook during a conversation; I'm talking about taking mental notes that you can record in a notebook for later reference. While this may sound clinical and too robotic to you, I can assure you that taking notes—like you're a student of your new friend—will serve you well in conversation and immediately form a special bond. For example, when I first learned how to write notes in the iPhone, I would often ask it to remind me about a friend's upcoming surgery date, work presentation, or travel if they had mentioned it in conversation with me. On that day, I could then call or text my friend to tell them I was thinking of them and praying for that particular event. I would also take notes of anniversaries and birthdays to celebrate and also difficult reminders of a death of a loved one. I could call on that day or send a gift to tell my friend I was thinking of her on that day.

I've secretly recorded these kinds of notes related to news students will share in class. If someone mentions an interview on a certain date for a job, for example, I'll write down the day. On that day, I'll ask in class how the interview went. They'll say, "Dr. H! You remembered. Wow!"

The power of taking notes surfaced even more powerfully after the death of my dear friend's mother. This precious woman—a grandmother to eight grandchildren—left behind a journal she kept that my friend recently found. She told me that in that journal, the grandmother kept detailed notes on each grandchild so she would know what to ask about during their phone calls or visits.

"What kinds of things did you find in the journal?" I asked.

"Everything. Things like their class schedules, music they liked, sports, new friendships, books they were reading. My mom would always know what to ask about and how to have a great conversation with each grandchild."

I tucked that wisdom away for the day I might become a grandmother. I think of that grandma journal on many days as I build new friendships. I added her technique to my own prayer journal where I write down the names of friends in my life who need prayer. I now take notes on their health concerns, their struggles, or their upcoming events so I remember to ask about them and pray for them. My students all know about my prayer journal, and they often ask if they can make their way into my prayers. My student hollered one day, "Dr. H! You know I'm an atheist, but you have to put me in that prayer journal. I need a job!" I did put that in my prayer journal, and the next month, I asked about the progress of his job search. Another student needed surgery after a dance injury. I told her I'd put her surgery in my prayer journal, and she started to cry.

"That's the nicest thing I think anyone has ever said to me while I've been at college," she said. After her surgery, I connected with her to find out how her recovery was going. She felt so loved and cared for.

As you limit distractions, take notes on your friends like you're a student of them. What are you learning about them? What upcoming events, anniversaries, or difficult days lie ahead for them?

Loving through Your Face

So far, we've learned about letting others talk, listening, and limiting distractions. The last tip involves our faces and what it means to build warm connections through a loving face. I'm in a front-facing profession. I stand in front of the public as both a conference speaker and a college professor. How I use my face matters deeply. As I began to research how to use my face effectively to build warm connections with others (especially my teen daughters and exhausted college students who don't really want to learn about verbs and semicolons at 9:00 a.m.), I discovered some fascinating research. In the research on how to "attune" to others well in conversation—so they feel connected to you—you want to practice a few tricks.

First, I learned that when you slightly elevate your eyebrows to "create a more open, smooth browline and forehead" it "[signals] receptivity rather than suspicion or judgment."[9] My face? I furrow my brows. I crinkle up my forehead. This is my thinking face, but it comes off as annoyed, judgmental, and angry. For years, people would ask me what was wrong, why I was so annoyed, or what made me so mad. I would say, "What? I'm just thinking deeply about what you're saying." After I read the research on attunement, I now regularly attempt to smooth my forehead muscles, unfurrow my brow, and raise my eyebrows to indicate interest, delight, and even joy. Try it. Raise your eyebrows and see how that feels. Now scrunch up your eyebrows and feel your wrinkled forehead. I even learned of a professional person who spent so many years with a furrowed brow that his clients always believed he was mad, impatient, and judging them. So deep were the furrows that he considered surgery to remove the angry look. While I don't think many of us can afford or even desire plastic surgery, it proves the point about how significant eyebrow expressions can be.

Second, I've learned that to create a loving face is actually counterintuitive. I once believed I should I tilt my head down and lean forward to demonstrate my interest and concern, but actually, leaning back and "tilting your chin up a degree or two and angling your neck slightly to expose your neck" shows openness and vulnerability.[10] It's a less intense and more receptive way to position your face.

I know this sounds weird, but I practice in the mirror. I tilt my chin up to expose my neck. Then, I raise my eyebrows and pretend

I'm responding to a friend in conversation. Try it with me if you want. *Remember what that feels like*. Now, in the next conversation, tilt the chin and raise the eyebrows. See what happens and how the conversation goes.

Consider how to express love, curiosity, and investment *through your face* as you listen to others.

When you think of improving on the basics of conversation, remember the Four Ls: *Let others talk. Listen for core values. Limit distractions. Love through your face.* But what if you cannot even start a conversation because of fear and self-consciousness? Don't worry, in the next chapter, we'll talk about that. You'll gain confidence to approach that new friend you cannot wait to meet, date, or simply improve your connection with others.

CHAPTER SEVEN

HANDLING FEAR AND SELF-CONSCIOUSNESS

Fear and excitement are actually the same feeling. Every single time you feel afraid, you can feel excited instead.

—Mel Robbins, American lawyer, television host, and motivational speaker

WHAT HOLDS YOU BACK from entering into that new conversation with that new person you want to get to know? What's keeping you from, right now, committing yourself to building warm connections with people in your life? You might take a book like this and memorize all the questions in the next chapter. You might even believe deeply in the Four Mindsets of a Loving Conversation (curiosity, positive regard, investment, and mutual sharing), but when it comes to the sharing part, you freeze up. You don't know what to say. You don't know how to carry a conversation where you share information about yourself.

I can tell you what most people fear more than anything else in the world. *Shame.* They fear exposure. They fear looking stupid. They become incredibly self-conscious that people are evaluating them.

You aren't alone if you feel this way, and you aren't alone in the terror regarding the fear of shame.

I studied the emotion of shame for five years for my doctoral degree at the University of Michigan in a dissertation that combined my love of literature with psychology. In particular, I wanted to investigate how shame really functions and if people writing about their shame experience found any positive results from exposing their weaknesses and vulnerabilities to other people. What I discovered was this: shame leads to intimacy. The more weakness, failure, vulnerability, and shortcomings you display in conversation, the more close conversation partners become. Why? It's because you can experience acceptance, unconditional love, and a common bond of shared weakness. You'll have that moment I mentioned previously from C. S. Lewis in *The Four Loves* about how friendship forms. You think you alone carry some personal burden, but Lewis explains the connection when you can say, "What? You too? I thought I was the only one."[1]

In my classes at Penn State, I teach my engineering students the professional skill of *self-disclosure*. In a classroom filled with more introverted, quiet, and even shy (by their own admission) computer engineers, for example, you might think inviting students to talk about their lives would feel like torture. Instead, with practice, these students find they feel connected with one another, seen and known, and more joyful. For class attendance, I ask a single question every day for students to self-disclose personal information. I do this for two reasons: self-disclosure is linked to better learning outcomes (it helps students become more creative and more receptive to learn), and the more they practice talking about themselves, the stronger their attachments with others will become. We find that we like each other. We know each other.

People Will Like You

Revealing something personal about yourself *makes people like you*. In a recent study, researchers report that "self-disclosure is the process of revealing personal information to another person, and it is a well-documented behavior that promotes liking and closeness within new relationships."[2] Coupled with my own research into shame and embarrassment, the more you share embarrassing or vulnerable things about yourself, the more people will like you, trust you, and connect with you.

In 2018, researchers from Harvard, Yale, Cornell, and Essex presented their findings on fear and self-consciousness in relationships in college students. The summary of this research offers great insight into how we might reframe how people think about us in conversation. We read this:

> Having conversations with new people is an important and rewarding part of social life. Yet conversations can also be intimidating and anxiety provoking, and this makes people wonder and worry about what their conversation partners really think of them. Are people accurate in their estimates? We found that following interactions, people systematically underestimated how much their conversation partners liked them and enjoyed their company, an illusion we call the *liking gap*. We observed the liking gap as strangers got acquainted in the laboratory, as first-year college students got to know their dorm mates, and as formerly unacquainted members of the general public got to know each other during a personal development workshop. The liking gap persisted in conversations of varying lengths and even lasted for several months, as college dorm mates developed new relationships. Our studies suggest that after people have conversations, they are liked more than they know.[3]

People like you. They like you more than you know. When you speak to someone in conversation, you become your "own greatest critic" and truly "overestimate how harshly others judge [you]" when in reality, your conversation partner is rarely judging you or aware of how self-conscious you feel.[4] Furthermore, this research on how much people actually like you in conversation revealed that participants "significantly underestimated how much others liked them."[5] What's even more troubling is the shier you are, the more likely you are to believe your conversation partner doesn't like you.[6]

> It might take some practice but try silencing the thoughts in your head that tell you you're awkward or boring or ridiculous.

What if you believed people liked you? What if you believed they weren't judging you in a conversation? What if you're forfeiting happiness by continuing to believe nobody enjoys conversations with you? Remember the concluding statement from the above research: "Conversations are a great source of happiness in our lives, but even more than we realize, it seems, as others like us more than we know."[7]

It might take some practice but try silencing the thoughts in your head that tell you you're awkward or boring or ridiculous. When you're talking to a friend, notice your self-evaluation and apply the truth: people like you. You're not annoying, boring, or ridiculous. And guess what? Even if you are, the very thing you're ashamed of will bond you with another person. You can also try this tip when you feel afraid or self-conscious: admit it. Tell your new friend or the stranger how you feel. You can say, "I know I'm so awkward! Ugh!" Or tell others that you're nervous. It's okay. Your conversation partner might feel the same way.

Other people need conversation. You offer a great gift to them when you enter into a conversation. Margaret Wheatley, an expert in community building, reminds us that "we can also take courage from the fact that many people are longing to be in conversation again. We are hungry for a chance to talk. People want to tell their story, and are willing to listen to yours. People want to talk about their concerns and struggles. Too many of us feel isolated, strange, or invisible. Conversation helps end that."[8]

People Like Personal Questions

As you think about sharing your life with others in conversations, you might still hesitate because you don't feel comfortable asking people personal questions about their lives. Perhaps your cultural or regional background taught you the virtue of staying reserved, not sharing personal information, and never asking questions that seem too personal. I've traveled enough throughout the United States (and have lived in the South, West, Midwest, and eastern parts of the country as a military daughter) to know that it can feel "rude" or "nosy" to ask someone a personal question. When I interviewed on a London radio station, the host reminded me that British people don't like to get too personal in conversation or share too much emotion. I laughed and said, "Well, I think you invited the wrong guest today!" So you might read this section and think, *I could never ask someone a personal question. I should keep my conversation to the weather, news, and sports.* Even more, you might come from a background of etiquette training that has advised, since as early as 1877, to *never ask someone any questions at all.*[9]

But consider the research on how people feel when you ask them "sensitive questions." Sure, it might feel risky to ask someone something private about themselves, and yes, as researchers admit, it could make the other person uncomfortable. But more likely, you will "initiate an engaging and meaningful conversation" and increase how much your conversation partner likes you by "enabling respondents to talk about themselves . . . which can increase . . . interpersonal closeness." Most significantly, researchers found that people "over-estimated the harmful effects of asking sensitive questions. Whether talking with a friend or with a new acquaintance, people do not mind answering sensitive questions nearly as much as those contemplating asking the sensitive questions anticipate," and these questions do not create a negative impression in the mind of the respondent.[10]

It Gets Less Scary and More Fun

Another way to ease your mind about self-consciousness and fear in approaching new people involves remembering the research about curiosity. Dr. Todd Kashdan helps us reframe the feelings of stress and anxiety as the excitement of "joyful exploration." He encourages us that "the highest level of anxiety [we] feel is always during the anticipation of something new. . . . Stick it out, and you see that the anxiety is manageable and can even be enjoyable."[11]

Each time you try to engage someone with a conversation question, it becomes easier. It simply takes practice. And the fear you feel? What if I told you that fear isn't always a bad thing? I received two pieces of life-changing advice regarding fear and self-consciousness—one from an actress and one from a wise mentor. When I began my public-speaking career, I wondered how I would keep working in such a fearful and nerve-wracking profession. I was once the type of public speaker who made myself physically sick with fear and self-consciousness. I hated that nauseating feeling before stepping out onto a stage. I almost quit booking events because of the fear. Before one event, an actress in attendance asked me how I was handling the stress of the big events at which I spoke. When I confessed how terrible my stomach felt and how I wasn't doing so well with my nerves, she put her hand on my arm and looked me straight in the eyes.

"You're misinterpreting that," she said calmly. "It's not fear and self-consciousness. It's adrenaline. It's a good thing. What you're experiencing—that sick-to-your-stomach feeling—is focusing your mind, making you sharp and alert, and keeping you connected to the moment. That feeling you hate? That feeling is your *best friend.*"

That feeling you have in starting a conversation? That rush of adrenaline and self-consciousness? It's your best friend. It's focusing you. It's not fear—it's the excitement of that joyful exploration.

Next, I met with a wise woman who asked how she could pray for me. I cried out, "I hate public speaking. And I think it's what God wants me to do. But I'm so afraid and self-conscious."

> *That feeling you have in starting a conversation? That rush of adrenaline and self-consciousness? It's your best friend. It's focusing you.*

"I don't understand," she said and tilted her head up in thought. "Aren't you a professor? Don't you stand in front of groups of people in a classroom all day long?"

"Yes," I said. "But that's *teaching.* That's not speaking. And I love teaching."

"What if you saw speaking as teaching and not speaking? Change the metaphor."

Her words forever changed my public speaking career. Speaking felt all about performance. Teaching felt like a gift I gave to an audience, something where the topic was the center, not me. I didn't matter; the content did. Talking to other people involves this reframing. It's not a performance or a job review. It's not a make-or-break thing. It's joyful exploration. It's excitement.

Do It by Faith

What if nothing I've written helps you? What if you're still struggling and cannot imagine approaching a new friend or starting a warm and loving conversation with a neighbor? Well, in this case (and really, in all cases), we do it *by faith.* We're finally doing something in our life that requires real faith because we're awkward and terrified.

Yesterday, I found myself walking to my classroom at Penn State about thirty minutes early. I like to go early so I can connect with students who join me to listen to music, hang out in the classroom, or study. In fact, I joke that my whole teaching philosophy is "Go Early."[12] Way ahead of me, I see my student walking toward my building. I see him holding his typical Starbucks iced coffee—which astonishes me in the snowy weather—in one hand and his phone in the other. I quicken my pace, my black snow boots pounding the gray sidewalk and I fly past bare trees, benches, and campus buildings. I'm about to holler his name and begin a conversation, but then I feel scared. I'm suddenly self-conscious. I feel so awkward, old, and out of place. My thoughts assault me: *What would I say? Does he want to talk to his professor? Aren't I just overwhelming and too much for students? Why do I even try to connect with people? Ugh! I'm doomed to a lonely life! What's wrong with me?*

But I had just read Hebrews 11:6 about living by "faith" and how "without faith it is impossible to please God" (NIV). I thought about having a conversation "by faith" because I certainly didn't want to if I lived by my emotions or sense of confidence. This wasn't going to happen in my own strength or by my own conversational talent. Could I call out that student's name "by faith" even though I felt shy and afraid? Could I do it?

I took a deep breath.

Conversations by faith. Okay. Okay. Okay. God can do this. Here I go.

"Malik! Malik! Hello!" I call out across the bleak, snowy campus.

Malik dramatically stops, swings around, and greets me with the biggest smile. He extends his arms wide as if he could hug me. I'm awkwardly running to catch up to him.

"Dr. H!" he hollers. "How are you?"

"I'm great!" I say, wheezing because I'm so out of shape. "You?"

"A bit stressed out."

"Your thesis? How is that coming?"

"It's okay." I notice he doesn't offer many words. I try another category.

"How was your Thanksgiving break? Did you absolutely feast?"

"Yes! I'm an only child, so I'm completely spoiled. I ate and slept and did nothing. It was perfect."

"What did you eat? Tell me everything," I said as we cheerfully walked on to the classroom. "I gotta hear about your spoiled life." By the time we were settled in our seats, I had shared about my own Thanksgiving and my favorite foods (mashed potatoes and stuffing, while Malik was all about sweet potatoes and pumpkin pie).

I continued to reach out to students that day "by faith" even when I felt self-conscious, awkward, and old. Later that afternoon, after a pack of students left my office, one lingered just to talk. She didn't have class for another thirty minutes, so she wanted to *just talk*. She said, "I just want you to know you're the only professor I talk to. The only professor. Nobody else asks or even knows anything about me. You ask about me." She leaned back in the chair, crossed her arms behind her head, and waited for my next question. And I asked more and more by faith.

Conversations "by faith" become exciting and supernatural. I first learned this concept several months before my snowy encounter with Malik. A fellow ministry worker with Cru connected with me at a conference last spring and asked if we could have lunch. She's more reserved and introverted. She listens more than she asks questions or talks. She'd even told me years before that she doesn't like to talk about emotions or deep, intellectual things. How would this lunch go? Would she start the conversation? Would I?

As we sat down to eat chicken salad sandwiches and salty pickles, she tilted up her head with a confidence I hadn't observed before. She said, "I asked God to help me think of the perfect question to ask you about your life, and a great one came to mind." She told me she prays about conversational questions. I love that. I love that it's conversation by faith, led by God.

Guess what she asked me? Something nobody has ever asked me. Something I secretly wanted to talk about but never had the chance to.

She asked this: "How have you been handling all the attention you get from your writing, speaking, and public presence? How do you feel about it?"

I loved this question because it engaged me volitionally (how I handle it), emotionally (how I feel), and socially (all the attention from people). I didn't just want to talk about this; I *needed* to talk about it. And she wanted to listen. I talked about the joys of it, like traveling for speaking events and meeting so many new people, but also the downsides of lonely hotel rooms, long airport layovers, and people who want you to spiritually counsel them all the time to the point where you're exhausted. I talked about coming to events and people approaching me—not because they wanted to get to know me, but because they wanted a connection to my agent and publisher. That hurts me.

"Have you ever had to deal with anything like this?" I asked. She couldn't relate at all, in any way, and we laughed about her choosing a private, hidden life. I asked her what she loves about that kind of life, and we had one of the most memorable and connected conversations I've had in many years. By the end, we were both encouraged in our callings, excited about growing to persevere through the downsides of our callings, and marveling about God's unique gifting of each of us—the Three Fresh Goals of a great conversation.

My friend taught me to have *conversations by faith*. When I'm afraid and self-conscious, I pray and ask God to lead me. I also remember that my conversation could be a great gift to a lonely person who needs to connect just as much as I do. As we all do.

CHAPTER EIGHT

THE SIX CONVERSATIONS

*It's hard to resist a generous question. We all have it
in us to formulate questions that invite honesty, dignity,
and revelation. There is something redemptive and
life-giving about asking a better question.*

—Krista Tippett, American journalist in *Becoming Wise*

*When I want to really get to know someone, I ask three
questions. People's answers to these give me great insight into
someone's heart. The questions are: What do you dream about?
What do you sing about? What do you cry about?*

—John Maxwell

MAYBE YOU'RE WONDERING why it took me so long to get to the practical part of this book—perhaps the very reason you purchased this book. You want the skills! You want the good stuff of immediate application! Well, I know this: if you have all the great questions without the foundational mindsets that undergird these questions, you'll come off as some kind of rapid-fire interviewer. You'll carry around questions like rocks you throw into the pond of someone's heart; you might get some ripples of a conversation, but ultimately, the question will land at the bottom of the water with no lasting impact. I know several people who study how to ask great questions to help you improve leadership. I read their books. I know they've discovered great questions. I've been on the receiving end of these great questions. But what I've realized as I've researched this book is this:

Questions alone don't work.

Our capacity to enter into loving conversation depends first on the Four Mindsets (being curious, believing the best, expressing concern, and mutual sharing) and the Three Fresh Goals (encouraging, helping growth, and marveling). Once positioned within this new framework, you can launch into a revolutionary new program of asking questions in the categories below that lead to endless permutations of more and more kinds of loving connection.

You'll gain confidence in starting conversations. You'll know where to go next in a conversation. You'll know where to linger and where to abandon certain trajectories. You'll know how to connect. And your life will change forever from lonely, disconnected, insecure, and even unhealthy to living in richer communities of deep connection, security, and well-being. Let me answer two key questions first:

WHY DO GOOD QUESTIONS MATTER SO MUCH? AND WHY THESE SIX CATEGORIES?

Did you know that when you ask someone a question, his or her brain changes? In fact, a question causes the brain to "get active as it reflects, releasing serotonin."[1] And when you ask someone their opinion about something, you offer them a uniquely pleasurable experience. Researchers show how, when asked to offer their opinion about something, participants showed on an MRI "increased neural activity in the areas of the brain associated with reward and pleasure."[2] I like to think of good conversations as a gift to a person's brain and a way to bless them. I remember community expert Margaret Wheatley's words: "Good questions—ones that we care about and that we want to answer—call us outward and to each other. They are an invitation to explore, to venture out, to risk, to listen, to abandon our positions. Good questions help us become both curious and uncertain, which is always the road that opens us to the surprise of new insight."[3] Good questions bring joy to a person's heart.

When I teach my students the professional skill of asking meaningful questions—those that move beyond sports, news, and weather—I remind them that it might indeed feel awkward to move beyond small talk or chit-chat. In a recent report delightfully called "Forget Small Talk: Why Emotionally Intelligent People Embrace the Rule of the Awkward Conversation, Backed by Science," the author recounts the research published in the *Journal of Personality and Social Psychology*. Researchers created awkward conversations between strangers. It turns out, even strangers feel happier and more connected to one another when invited to answer questions that at first will feel awkward to answer.[4] We might have not wanted to answer these questions either, but in the end researchers proved how happy and connected conversation partners felt toward each other. The questions included topics about gratitude, what truth you're searching for, and this statement which I love: "If you were going to become a close friend with the other participant, please share what would be important for him or her to know."[5] While participants might have felt embarrassed or nervous, they very quickly became comfortable talking.

> *Questions, then, provide the foundation for how a conversation begins and continues, and they create feelings of pleasure and connectedness.*

Spark Questions: Questions, then, provide the foundation for how a conversation begins and continues, and they create feelings of pleasure and connectedness. In fact, if we wish to become truly excellent conversation partners (who doesn't?) we might follow the advice of relationship expert Vanessa Van Edwards (self-described "recovering awkward person"), bestselling author of *Captivate: The Science of Succeeding with People.* In her article on "How to Have and Hold Dazzling Conversation with Anyone," Van Edwards offers the tips I've mentioned so far (believing the best, mutual sharing, raising your eyebrows, having a purpose), but she provides excellent question-asking strategies. She calls these questions "sparks" that help someone feel joy. She writes, "Sparks usually come from asking someone about topics that trigger dopamine. This is a chemical that makes us feel excited and engaged. I recommend triggering dopamine by bringing up topics that will help someone feel joy." She includes her favorite "sparks" of asking about upcoming vacations, passion projects, the best part of someone's week, or even whether they've tried any new restaurants.[6] But Van Edwards's favorite question? It's this: *How 'bout you?* She reminds us to always bounce the conversation back to your partner with that question to invite mutual sharing—the fourth mindset of a great conversation.

Asking others "spark" questions—those questions that bring up positive emotions in the other person—helps conversations begin. And beginning joyful conversations matters now more than ever in light of the research of pandemic loneliness and disconnection, especially in the college-aged population. So vital are good questions now that, in a recent email correspondence to parents of college students returning for the holidays, the Dean of Students of the University of Pittsburgh wrote a list of questions to encourage rich dialogue. Some of her spark questions included asking about favorite professors, new friends, and highlights from the semester.[7]

Numbers Questions: Spark questions help ease people into a conversation, but I recently learned something that makes a conversation question exceedingly simple to answer. You can ask a question that involves a number. This trick refers to a "conversation hack" offered by Jerry Seinfeld. Van Edwards explains how Seinfeld engages with people after a comedy performance. Because even Seinfeld gets nervous and can't figure out what question to ask people to start a conversation, he learned to ask a "numbers-based question" as the easiest way to get people talking. Questions with numbers for the answer help people get into a conversation if they are nervous. *How long have you lived here? How long did it take you to get here? How many years have you been in your career?*[8] With a numbers question, you've started a conversation, and the next step involves any one of the Six Conversations. I do this with my students all the time. If a new student arrives to class, I'll often ask a numbers question like, "How many classes do you have today?"

My favorite numbers question, however, I learned from the article "How to Become a Master at Talking to Strangers" by Joe Keohane, who shares the wisdom of Georgie Nightingall, the founder of Trigger Conversations, a London-based training program to help people connect. She suggests a unique use of numbers in conversation by inviting a partner to talk about what kind of day they are having on a scale of 1 to 10. I used this with cashiers, my teen daughters, and even my husband. The best part isn't that first question. It's the next one: Whatever they answer, you say, "What would it take to get you a 10?"[9] (Or if they've answered "10," I ask, "What made it a 10?") Finally, I also use numbers to get to storytelling in conversation. When I find out what someone does for a living, I can ask, "How long have you wanted to do that?" They'll often tell the story of a childhood dream or the moment they realized a vocational calling.

Nightingall reminds us that questions matter for how people enjoy your company in a conversation based on a series of studies in

2017. We read how psychologist Karen Huang and her colleagues realized that "people who ask more questions, particularly follow-up questions, are better liked by their conversation partners."[10] Those partners felt that those asking questions were better listeners, more understanding, and more caring.[11]

BUT WHY SIX CONVERSATIONS?

Now to the good part. Once you understand the value of asking a good question, you need to know where to go next. What I've discovered is so simple you'll want to start using the technique immediately. Think of the six dimensions of what it means to be human. We are social, emotional, physical, cognitive, volitional, and spiritual. Once you ask a question—any question at all to start a conversation—you can enjoy endless permutations of follow-up questions to produce a thrilling, close, and joyful conversation. We'll examine each category in detail next, but let me first give you a quick overview. Imagine you've asked your friend what she had for breakfast. It might go like this:

"Hello! It's good to see you! Did you get a good breakfast this morning?"

"Oh, hey. Yeah. Um, just coffee."

"Coffee? Cool." Long pause. Oh no! What do you say next? How do you have a real conversation? Simple. Move through the six dimensions of being human and choose your next question.

Did you see any friends in the coffee shop? (social)

Are you someone who immediately feels better after that first sip like me? (emotional)

How many cups can you drink a day without it affecting your sleep or nerves? (physical)

What made you think to go to that coffee place instead of the other one? (cognitive)

What did you order? (volitional)

Does the coffee include any kind of ritual for well-being? I drink coffee when I pray and read my Bible. You? (spiritual)

I've learned to move down the possibilities of the six conversation questions, and they inevitably open up a new dimension for connecting. No matter what I ask about, I can choose a category for the next question and see what kinds of connections form between us. And I keep in mind the Four Mindsets and the Three Fresh Goals. I continue the conversation until we've arrived at encouragement, growth, or marveling. As you read the descriptions and examples of the Six Conversations, think of which category most interests you.

1. SOCIAL

People like to talk about the people in their lives. They like to answer questions about their children, roommates, spouses, students, clients, and so on. We are social creatures, and connection with others about the people in our lives works as one of the easiest kinds of conversations.

Questions for Starting a Social Conversation:
1. What new friends have you made recently?
2. How do you enjoy your friends showing support to you?
3. How are things going with your [roommate, family members, pet]?
4. Do you have any upcoming plans with friends?
5. Which person in your life right now is a role model to you? Who do you think you're a role model to?

6. For what reason have people been seeking your input or advice lately?

7. What's a question you like people to ask you right now?

8. Who is the oldest person you know? Who is the youngest person you know?

9. If you could invite someone new to dinner this week, who would you want to have over?

10. What do you value most in friendship right now?

I have two teen daughters, and they love talking about their friends. I can ask questions in any other conversational category, and I'll get annoyed, one-word answers. But as soon as I start asking about their friends, the conversation explodes with joy, laughter, and stories of drama or funny experiences. Even if I start with a question from another category like, "How are you sleeping?" (physical)—and they say, "Fine," if I follow with, "Which roommate gets the least amount of sleep?" Or "What kinds of things do you like doing with your friends late at night?" the conversation moves easily.

With my friends, sometimes I start a conversation with, "What friends have you seen lately?" For my friends who work a lot, I ask, "Have you had enough social time lately? What have you been doing with friends and what do you *wish* you were doing with friends?" I love asking my students this question because I can quickly find out who loves sports, who loves boardgames, who loves going shopping, who wants to travel, or who loves quiet conversations in coffee shops. I like to share that, right now, I wish I was hiking or talking with friends about God.

With people who feel distant, cold, or unable to connect with you for any reason, you can ask, "Which question do you like your friends to ask you?" or even "What do you like to talk about with your friends?" I tried this question with an extremely reserved and withdrawn student. We were walking to my office in complete silence. He finally said, "I just don't like to talk to people."

I said, "Well, if you *had* to talk about something—if you had to be social and talk to friends—what would you wish people would talk about?" He paused for an uncomfortably long time. He looked at his feet. I waited. Finally, an answer:

"Pokémon."

"You mean the card game or the video game?"

"Both."

"How did you first start playing Pokémon? How old were you?"

He beamed! The entire walk from our classroom to my office across campus, I learned about Pokémon. We talked and talked about this game, who he plays with, and why he loves it. I wanted the whole story. He wouldn't stop talking about it. I smiled and said, "Do you hate talking to me about this? You don't like to talk to people, but you're talking to me."

"That's different," he said. "You asked about Pokémon."

Best Tip for asking questions about people: Use the word "story" in your question. "What's the story behind how you met your [roommate, spouse, best friend]?" Our brains love narrative, and we are naturally drawn to storytelling in the social category.

Questions for Continuing a Social Conversation:

As you've asked your first question in conversation—about anything at all—you can follow up with questions about other people, even if your first question involves sports or the weather. Ask questions involving *people.* You'll never get stuck knowing where to go next in a conversation if you think about the social dimension of being human. Consider these ten questions:

1. Who else did you see there? Who else was involved?
2. Did you turn to any particular person for help? Have you told anyone else?
3. What have you been learning about friendships?
4. Why did you pick that person to be with?
5. Did other people experience that too? How were they impacted?
6. How were your other relationships impacted?
7. Did this change how you viewed yourself?
8. Did this change how you viewed God?
9. What do you enjoy most about that person or group?
10. What's the easiest/hardest thing about that relationship?

Try it! Start with a mundane, surface level question, and see how quickly you can warmly and lovingly connect with someone in the social category of question asking. Remember to stay curious, believe the best, become invested, and share your life.

Best Tip for Continuing a Social Conversation: When someone shares anything with you, try this: "Wow—that's cool! Who else was there?"

2. EMOTIONAL

I'll never forget the day my neighbor's dog died. The owner, retired military who now served as a professor, was the one to take his beloved dog to the vet on the day the sweet dog died. A few days later, our families enjoyed roasting marshmallows around a fire pit together. As we started the conversation, I decided to take a risk and ask an *emotional* question. I knew veterans often don't like talking about hard emotions, but I wanted to communicate our love for him and the dog by asking, "How did you deal with the emotions of losing your dog that day?"

He paused and then told us the deeply distressing story of his final moments with his dog. As he became more emotional, I said, "I'm sorry I asked about how emotional it was for you." He said, "Don't apologize. I *want* to talk about this. I *need* to talk about this."

Sometimes people need to talk about their emotions, yet we often don't know how to ask loving questions in this category. We also think that people will be offended or won't have the maturity to simply say, "I'm not ready to talk about this right now." I'm learning to regularly include questions that allow people to talk about their feelings—both positive and negative.

I'm also learning to move beyond "How are you?" or "How was your weekend?" If you notice, the weak verbs (are and was) reflect existential states of being. The brain cannot easily find a category to answer that question, so we'll always hear "fine" or "good." But if you add a precise, strong verb, in that question, you'll find your conversation partner opens up. For example, I recently attended a baby shower where several coworkers were reuniting after a long summer apart. I noticed that not many people were having conversations. I heard the question with the weak verb over and over again: *How was your summer? Fine. It was fine.*

I decided to try the strong verb and see what happened. So I asked my colleague, "Did anything *surprise* you about your summer?"

"Surprise me?" she repeated. "Oh, I like that question. Yes, in fact, let me tell you about what happened when . . ."

Now, instead of "How was your weekend?" I insert a strong verb like this in the emotional category of conversation.

Did anything *surprise* (confuse, disappoint, excite) you about your weekend?

I use the strong verb trick with my daughter about her schoolwork. Instead of "How was the exam?" I now ask, "Did anything surprise you about the exam? Did anything make you happy about that exam?"

I love it when I come home from a trip because my husband applies the strong verb trick and no longer asks, "How was your trip?"

I'd always say "fine," and move on. But when he picks me up from the airport and says, "Tell me about this trip! What surprised you?" I open up with all my feelings and great stories from the weekend.

Think of these questions to begin or continue a conversation:

Questions for Starting an Emotional Conversation:

1. What things have you been truly grateful for recently?
2. What's been stressing you out or bothering you lately?
3. What's been going well for you? What are you celebrating?
4. Where are you feeling you need courage lately?
5. What's been the emotion you're feeling most these days?
6. Have you felt any joy lately?
7. What are you looking forward to this week?
8. Do you have any good news?
9. How are you feeling about your work, family, friendships, schedule, etc.?
10. Is today a happy day or a hard day?

Questions for Continuing an Emotional Conversation:

1. What has this [any topic] been like for you?
2. What does that feel like emotionally? Is it fear or sadness? Is it anger?
3. Did this stir up any old emotions or give you a new emotional experience?
4. What does this make you long for?
5. Does this bring up feelings of nostalgia?
6. On a scale of 1 to 10, how emotional did that make you?
7. Were you surprised about the emotions that brought up in you?
8. Has any emotion you've experienced about this felt irrational or strange?
9. Is it hard/easy for you to experience those emotions?
10. Why do you think it made you feel that way?

Best Tip for Emotional Conversations: As someone shares anything with you about his or her life, you can reflect and say, "Wow. That's a big deal. What did that feel like to you?"

3. PHYSICAL

Most people forget the power of asking about how others are doing *physically*. People love to talk about their bodies, their physical spaces, and their physical experiences. Some of my most connected conversations begin when I ask someone if they are feeling any pain in their bodies, how they slept the night before, or what they ate for breakfast. It seems simple, but we forget the pleasure of talking about the body and what the body enjoys—sleeping, tasting delicious food, exercising our bodies, listening to music, seeing beautiful sights, touching comforting textures, and building physical spaces in our lives. Think of the five senses: we can ask about what people have seen, heard, felt, tasted, and smelled.

I recently endured three surgeries in the span of one month (kidney stones and a surgery to remove fibroids). The emergency kidney stone surgeries felt traumatic and scary, so I enjoyed people asking me questions about my emotions and also the social aspect of the surgery. I needed to talk about how lonely it felt during COVID to not have my husband with me. I needed to talk about the nurses and doctors I met. But, as I shared these things in conversation, I secretly wished people would ask me about the physical aspects of it all. I wanted to talk about the pain, the stitches, the medication, and the recovery. All of it. I wanted to talk about all the gory physical details, like removing the stent or the glue on the stitches. Since I remembered wishing people would ask me about the physical details, I now start there when I meet up with a friend who has just had surgery or is recovering from any kind of illness. They light up when I say, "Tell me all about what it was like for you physically. Tell me what was happening to your body.

What was it like? Give me all the details."

I also recently needed to connect professionally with someone I considered shier, highly technically minded, and reserved in conversation. During one of our meetings together, I tried and tried to figure out a way to connect, but I only received one-word answers as I asked about his feelings about his semester (emotional) or how he was enjoying his students and colleagues (social).

"Fine," he'd say. "It's fine."

Silence.

Then I remember the dimension of being human that involves physical spaces and our physical pleasures like food. So I tried again. I simply asked one question that kept us in vibrant, connected conversation for the next forty-five minutes. My question? I said this:

"I heard you live outside of town with a lot of land. Do you garden? Tell me about how you physically handle all that land!"

He lit up. I learned all about his winter seeds sprouting in his basement. I learned about his heirloom flower bulbs. I learned about his garden design. I stayed curious. I stayed invested. And I shared about my own plum trees I grew from seed. He stayed curious. He was invested. I gained so much advice about my growing plum orchard. We laughed and shared about gardening successes and failures.

But it didn't end there. I remembered to keep asking about physical spaces and things people enjoy physically. So I said, "Hey—you must live out near that new cidery. Have you been? Do you enjoy apple cider?"

Before I knew it, he and his wife invited me and my husband for an evening at the cidery.

I never felt awkward around my friend again.

Finally, during one semester, I didn't feel as close to my students or that they were connected strongly in community. I decided to ask about their physical bodies with questions like, "How are you taking care of yourself? How are you sleeping?" The students loved my questions about sleep so much that we decided to create a good-night-sleep challenge to get eight hours of sleep. We even reported each day on our sleep and offered strategies for enjoying a better night's sleep. A student came up to me after class and said, "Dr. H, I have felt so lonely. When I come to your class, it's the best part of my day. I love talking to everyone. Your questions are a lifeline for me. Thank you. And my parents say thanks, too."

Questions for Starting a Physical Conversation:

1. How have you been taking care of yourself lately?
2. What have you been doing to relax?
3. What's the story behind the shirt (jewelry, shoes, hat) you're wearing?
4. What music (social media, movies, shows) have you been listening to or watching lately?
5. Tried any new restaurants? What are you making for dinner tonight?
6. What's your exercise routine these days? Have you taken any good hikes?
7. What's your favorite place in your house or workspace right now? For younger conversation partners, ask about dorms, apartments, bedrooms.
8. How did you sleep last night?
9. Are you feeling any pain in your body? What hurts?
10. Are you doing any home improvement projects?

Questions for Continuing a Physical Conversation:

1. What did that do to your body?
2. Did that impact your sleep at all?
3. Did that refresh you or exhaust you?

4. What's your next home improvement plan or are you planning anything new for your dorm, apartment, bedroom? Any garden plans?

5. Did that feel cozy to you? What textures were involved?

6. What made that taste so good to you?

7. Did you see anything beautiful there?

8. What do you remember hearing? What did it sound like?

9. What's your plan to take care of your body next?

10. How are you designing your work or study space?

I love this category because no matter how a conversation begins, you can always ask a physical follow-up question. If I start a conversation with, "Hey! How are you? Are you feeling good in your body today?" that's an obvious physical conversation. But imagine you've asked someone how their weekend was. I've bolded my questions so you can observe how easy this category of questions actually is:

"How was your weekend? Any fun plans?"

"Yeah, we visited my dad in New Jersey."

(Note: At this point, I can ask a social, emotional, cognitive, volitional, spiritual question, but I choose physical. See what happens.)

"Was it a refreshing visit? Or did it drain you?"

"I'm so drained. I'm exhausted."

"Oh, man! I'm sorry! **Where does exhaustion show up in your body?"**

"Wow—that's a good question. Believe it or not, it's my back. I have plenty of energy, but my back is killing me."

"Lower or upper?"

"Lower. I'm dying."

"Oh no. Is this going to impact your work today?"

"I'm okay. I can take a half day. But back pain is the worst."

"I know what you mean. That happened to me last year after a road trip. I was on my back for three days."

"What did you do to feel better?"

And voilà! *Connection.*

Finally, I love the uniqueness of asking physical questions. People often don't expect them, but they end up opening wonderful (and often needed) conversations. They also give us something tangible to discuss in the face of tragedy. I consulted a trauma expert who travels to communities devastated by natural disasters. When she meets with suffering people, she often asks this question, "Where are you feeling the pain in your body?" She wants to know if they want to talk about their emotions or if they need to talk about what's happening physically to them. I used this advice when I recently met with a grieving friend. I wasn't sure what to ask her, so I sat with her, cried, and then asked, "How are you feeling the grieving in your body?" She loved this question. Nobody had ever asked her this, and she wanted to talk about all the trembling and nausea she was feeling.

You can also ask people this question who've just received great news or an exciting opportunity. Instead of asking, "How did that feel?" from the emotional category, you can ask, "What did it feel like physically to get that news?" You'll find your friends might say, "Good question! Let me tell you how I was shaking with joy and sweating like a teenager in love!"

When you ask about the physical side of life, it opens up so many new possibilities for connected conversation. I also love the physical questions to help people think differently about the connection between their bodies and deeper, spiritual connections. If someone is complaining that they don't feel beautiful, I love asking the question award-winning journalist and radio host Krista Tippett asks in her book *Becoming Wise.* Tippett expertly asked her guests the most powerful questions to generate meaningful conversation. She loves to ask, "What are you doing when you feel the most beautiful?"[12]

Best Tip for Physical Conversations: No matter what someone shares with you, think about how it impacts physical space or their physical body. How will that affect your space? Your body?

4. COGNITIVE

So far, we've talked about three go-to categories of conversation so you can start and continue *any* conversation. If you feel stuck or get that awkward feeling that there's silence and you're not feeling connected, remember you can ask a social, emotional, or physical question. These questions invite others easily into conversation without much effort. For our next category of conversation—cognitive—we'll find we start to arrive at complexity, depth, and meaning quickly. The cognitive category empowers your conversation partner to think and respond thoughtfully. This category works really well if you're in a problem-solving situation, if your friend is complaining about something or in a hard spot, or if they don't seem interested in talking about their social, emotional, or physical lives. I name this the cognitive category (rather than intellectual) because this isn't about being smart, academic, or bookish. It's about connecting over what we're thinking about.

I love the cognitive category of conversation. Sometimes we get stuck in our own thoughts and feel increasingly lonely and disconnected from others. When you ask a question that engages a thought process about how the mind is working, consider the rich blessing of it. When I ask cognitive questions, my friends feel honored, affirmed, and empowered. In simple terms, the cognitive category refers to the mental process part of being human. These are conversations involving how we are thinking, what we are learning, and how we find meaning in the world around us.

Questions for Starting a Cognitive Conversation:

1. What are you learning lately?
2. How are you making sense of [news, an event, anything happening in their world]?
3. Have you had to make any hard decisions lately?
4. What thought keeps going through your head you cannot get rid of?
5. What have you been curious about lately?
6. Are you currently working on an unanswered question in life?
7. What have you been pondering today?
8. Are you thinking differently about this [news, event, anything happening] from most people?
9. What has been your favorite thing to think about lately?
10. What do you think about this?

I often like to start with the cognitive category because I hang out with a lot of professors who like to talk about their ideas. Often, I'll start with a greeting and mention something happening on campus. Even if it's about a recent basketball game or campus event, I start the conversation with, "What did you think about that game? How did you make sense of it?" But it's not just academics who like talking about their thoughts. I love asking children about what they've been curious about or how they are making sense of the world. Based on the advice of a trauma expert, I learned that in stressful situations where I don't know what to say—like when I'm with a hurting friend or seeing someone who just received terrible news—I put my arm around them and say, "This is so tough. I know you are overwhelmed, and your thoughts might be spinning. What thought keeps going through your mind that you can't get rid of?" This question blesses people who feel unable to get out of a certain thought pattern. Simply asking someone what's going on in their mind allows them to talk to someone and ease that stress.

You can continue any conversation using these follow-up questions in the cognitive category. Children in particular love these questions.

Questions for Continuing a Cognitive Conversation:

1. Why do you think that is?
2. Is this a new idea for you? Who or what inspired it? How did you come up with that?
3. How are you making sense of this?
4. How are you connecting this experience to other areas of your life?
5. What are some different ways to think about this?
6. Do you think differently about this from most people?
7. Did this make you ask another question or think about something else?
8. What new information or fresh understanding are you needing or seeking about this?
9. How long have you been thinking about this? Or, When did you first start thinking about this?
10. Is this your favorite thing to think about? Is it the least favorite? What helps you stop thinking about it? What makes you start thinking about it?

Best Tip for Cognitive Conversations: When having cognitive conversations, you can always simply ask, "What do you think?" and then spin off into other categories easily like this: Who else thinks like you do? Do you often talk to others about this (social)? Does that thought stir up a certain emotion for you (emotional)? Does that thought process make you feel stress in your body or upset your stomach? Do your thoughts ever impact your physical self (physical)? What choices did that open up for you (volitional)? Or, Did that connect to your religion (spiritual)?

5. VOLITIONAL

Last year, I began researching human volition (our ability to make choices and act upon them).[13] I was curious about the impact asking a single question had on both my children and my students. When either my daughter or a student was experiencing stress, anxiety about the future, or complaining about something, I would ask this question:

"What are your choices?"

The first time I used this question involved a child who was experiencing chronic nosebleeds. She never knew when they would come or what kind of classroom situation she'd be in. She was so fearful and nervous each day because she couldn't predict what would happen. Even though she was only a third grader at the time, I asked her, "Well, if your nose starts bleeding, what are your choices? You are never trapped in a situation. What could you choose to do?"

Suddenly, this child tilted her head up and raised her eyebrows. I could see her confidence rising as she pointed one little finger in the air and said, "I could keep tissues with me and excuse myself to the nurse."

"That's good. What else?"

"I could tell the teacher I might get a nosebleed and maybe give a signal or something."

"That's awesome."

Years later, I was talking with a teenager who felt trapped in a math class that was poorly taught and caused anxiety for every assignment. I tried the same question.

"What are your choices? You aren't trapped."

"I could hire a tutor. I could watch the lessons on YouTube from another teacher."

"Or?"

"I could switch into another math class."

"Then what? What would you do then?"

"Well, I'd have to make new friends and adjust to another teacher." Again, the anxiety left her as I watch the volitional part of her brain working. She felt empowered and in control of the situation.

When students or women in my ministry life begin to cry about a stressful or overwhelming situation, I can defuse the tension and angst as soon as I begin a volitional conversation. "That's so hard," I'll say. "What choices do you have now? What's your next step?"

What I love about the volitional category of conversation is how it empowers my friends. It gives them a real sense of agency. I also love how this category helps you quickly discern what people need, where they feel no sense of power or agency, and where they feel hopeless and trapped. You'll find the volitional category helpful as you serve other people, especially traditionally underrepresented or under-resourced groups. I recently asked a ministry expert in a major city how best to engage in racial reconciliation conversations and how best to minister to hurting members of minority communities, especially during the 2019–2021 years. She said this: "Ask people what they need that they cannot get. Ask them where they feel they have no choices. Then see how you can serve."

Asking another person, "Where in your life do you feel you have no choices?" isn't an easy conversation to have, and it's not the best for people who don't feel equipped or ready to handle what the answer could be. In this case, I often invite other people into this conversation so we, as a team, can enter in and help. I also know how to have resources ready if I'm in a situation where I feel a person is in danger to themselves or others.[14] With people who have endured a death of a loved one or a calamity of any kind, we can lovingly ask, "What are your small tasks today to get you moving? What if you drank more water today or took a short walk with me? Would you like to have lunch? Would you like to choose a dinner I could make and send over?" Helping hurting people make a choice for the day helps them feel more in control and less afraid.

Finally, I learned to empower people who regularly seek my advice as a spiritual counselor. Because I have written bestselling books in the inspirational market, people often approach me for counsel about their lives. After someone shares their story, they'll say, "What do *you* think I should do?" I always pause, look them in the eye, and say this:

"I think deep down, you know what you should do and what choice to make here. What do you think you should do?"

With tears in her eyes, one woman who had endured struggle after struggle and felt beaten down on all sides said she never had anyone honor her own decision-making abilities. She had never felt empowered to make a choice for her own life.

Tears of joy streamed down her face now. She smiled, and with sparkling eyes, she said, "I do. I know exactly what I want to do. I want to start my business." She slapped the table where we were sitting together.

"Okay then!" I replied, cheering her on. "What's your next step? What's the next choice?"

Sometimes (most of the time!) our friends need to feel empowered in conversation in the volitional category.

You can see the power of a volitional conversation in one of my favorite TikTok videos that's so beautiful it makes me cry (yes—I'm on TikTok!). The famous barber Vic Blends gives free haircuts on the street to random people as part of his ministry to the world. But it's not the haircut that's the only blessing. It's the *conversation*. I reached out to Vic to tell him how much I admired his conversational style and loving questions. In one particular video from September 30, 2021, Vic approaches a Kennesaw State college student and asks him if he can give him a free haircut. In a video viewed over 1.9 million times to date, we see Vic build the most loving and connected conversation. Vic sometimes uses profanity, so you might choose not to watch this video. I put Vic's volitional questions in bold so you can see them at work in a real conversation:

Vic: "You got some time for me?"

Stranger: "Yeah, I got you."

Vic: "Let's get it. All right, what is your name and what do you do?"

The young man shares his name and that he's a college student. He then shares his major. Then Vic asks: **"What made you choose that field?"** As the student shares his story and how he wants to "give people a voice," Vic asks, **"Has that been your goal the whole time?"** While Vic continues the conversation with some emotional questions (How are you liking college? Was COVID a rough year for you?), he returns to the volitional conversation and asks, **"What's the next step for you?"** Vic sprinkles in some loving, personal questions that relate to the physical (How has your culture shaped you?), but again, he naturally follows where the student likes to talk in conversation in the volitional realm. He then asks, **"What keeps you motivated?"**

Next, the conversation takes a deeply connected turn. As the student talks about poor motivation due to mental health issues, Vic ventures into the emotional category and asks, "Have you ever battled depression before?" As the student discusses turning his life over to God to get out of his depression, Vic asks a cognitive question: "When you look back on that time, what do you think about?" The student talks about how proud he is of that time, and Vic says, "I'm proud of you too!" Vic next asks another volitional question, **"What would you tell someone right now going through depression?"** This question seems to unlock the student's mind. He has advice to give. He can help people make great choices to emerge from depression. Here, Vic decides to share his own life and his own journey.

In the final moments, the man (once a stranger and now a friend) smiles and says, "One day, when I make it, I ain't forgetting you."

Vic says, "You already made it, bro!" And the conversation ends with encouragement and gratitude. They celebrate where God has brought them. They part ways saying, "I appreciate you so much, man."

One way to remember the volitional category is that it's all about choices and action. "What's next for you? What is your next action? What will you do? What made you do that?" It's often difficult to start a conversation with a volitional question (because they work so well as follow-up questions), but here are some questions to try after someone has shared initial information in conversation:

Questions for Starting a Volitional Conversation:

1. How have you chosen to spend your time lately?
2. What made you decide to get together today?
3. What's next for you today?
4. Are you working toward any goals today?
5. What caused that?
6. Have you had to make any interesting decisions yet today?
7. What's the next big decision coming up for you?
8. Did you decide to do that thing? Was that a good or bad decision for you?
9. What made you choose that great [outfit, coffee drink, outing, anything]?
10. What's your routine been like today?

When you're in any category of conversation, remember how volitional questions offer others a chance to feel in control, to exert agency, and to avoid feeling trapped. They also help people focus on goals. Volitional conversations happen most frequently with my achievement-driven colleagues at Penn State. They love these kinds of follow-up questions in conversation:

Questions for Continuing a Volitional Conversation:

1. Did that make you feel like you had no power? What did you do?
2. What's your next step? How can I help you with your next step?
3. What can you control here, and what is outside of your control?
4. What are your choices here?
5. How did you handle that?
6. What did/will you decide to do?
7. Is there something that you want to do that you haven't done yet?
8. Have you set any goals in that area yet?
9. What do you think is keeping you from that?
10. Do you have to make a decision about that right now?

Sometimes, when my friends feel overwhelmed and stressed out, it's because they know they have to make a decision about something. Serving as a friend who listens and asks questions in the volitional category means that you can naturally ask follow-up questions in all the other categories. With professors and students who I discover are in a decision-making process, I can ask these questions: "How are you thinking about this decision (cognitive)? Is this decision becoming hard on your body (physical)? Who else can we loop into this conversation for advice (social)? Can we pray and ask God for wisdom here (spiritual)? What emotions is this decision bringing up for you (emotional)?"

Best Tip for Volitional Conversations: No matter what someone shares with you about something they're doing, you can say, "Was that an easy choice?" or "How did you decide to do that?"

6. SPIRITUAL

I love talking about Jesus. In fact, most of my conversations inevitably end up in the spiritual realm; it's the way I feel closest with others.

When I meet you, I want to know your spiritual background, your current thoughts about God, and what you think about the soul, eternity, and supernatural things. I love talking about answers to prayer, insights from the Bible, or how others worship. It's the best part of conversation for me. Many people long to start or transition naturally to spiritual conversations, but they simply can't think of a good question to ask other people.

I've been asking people questions about God since the fifth grade. I remember asking my friends spiritual questions as we walked home from school. *Do you think about God? Do you wonder about heaven? Do you think God answers our prayers? Do you really think God made everything? Do you think we have guardian angels?*

My questions in this area felt endless in my mind, and thankfully, people around me loved talking about supernatural things. In fact, that's what we did most of all. During sleepover parties, people wanted to tell ghost stories and began pulling out games like fortune-telling, Tarot, and the popular Ouija board that I'm thankful I ran from. Back in the late 80s and early 90s, we were all reading Stephen King novels or *Scary Stories to Tell in the Dark*. We were wondering about demons and listening to the debates about whether Dungeons and Dragons was an evil game. Growing up in that culture meant people talked about spiritual things. I used to think that was a different time and teenagers don't think about things like that anymore, but when I ask my students what they love to watch and talk about, they report their fascination with horror movies and anything supernatural. They love talking about haunted places on campus or within the state of Pennsylvania. In fact, what concerned me most as a Christian last year as I taught highly academic and brilliant honors students was the interest in and practice of witchcraft. My students talk about rehabilitating ancient witchcraft practices including spells and divination. Those who wouldn't say they align with actual witchcraft like to talk about what seems less harmless to them: astrology, manifesting, energy healing, and crystals. Students use runes and spells before tests. They explain their restless mood or bad fortune by saying things like, "Of course! Venus is in retrograde!" If you think that there's no spiritual activity or interest in the supernatural happening among young people today, I can assure you this is not the case.

Naturally, this opens the door for spiritual conversations nearly every day. I report this climate on the college campus to let you know that people *enjoy* talking about spirituality. It's on their minds. It's part of their lives in some form. And they have questions about it.

When I first started entering the spiritual category of conversation, I enjoyed pretending people around me were already Christians because it made me feel more authentic and less strategic. I didn't want conversation about God to feel like a sales pitch. I regularly engaged my neighbors in conversations about God, and I would share what Jesus was doing in my life. I would turn to one professor and say, "Does it bother you that I talk so much about Jesus?" I'll never forget what she said.

"No! I want to hear everything you have to say about Him."

I've asked people that same question many times in the last twenty years. Does it bother you that I talk so much about Jesus? Never in nearly two decades has anyone said yes. Nobody is bothered when someone brings up something precious to their heart. It's the richest, deepest, and most rewarding conversation to share about our spiritual lives.

Questions for Starting a Spiritual Conversation:

1. Have you been thinking about spiritual or supernatural things lately?
2. Have you started (or are you continuing) any spiritual rituals lately?

3. Is your relationship with God something that's important to you?

4. Are you a churchgoer?

5. What was your religious background growing up? What's your religious heritage from your grandparents or great-grandparents?

6. Do you think the Bible has anything to offer anymore?

7. Do you consider yourself on a spiritual journey?

8. Do you have anything going on that I can pray for?

9. What does your spiritual tradition say about Jesus?

10. Do you think this is a spiritual problem?

Questions for Continuing a Spiritual Conversation:

1. Did you experience the presence of God in that moment? Where do you think God was?

2. What do you think God is doing in this situation?

3. If you were to ask me to pray about this, what would you want me to pray for?

4. How is your religion helping you deal with this?

5. Who or what did you turn to for meaning or how to make sense of it all?

6. Has this surfaced any spiritual questions for you?

7. Did that make you wonder about eternal things or things beyond just our material experience?

8. Do you think that was a coincidence or is something else going on?

9. What is keeping you from going back to your religious tradition?

10. Did that make you want to cry out to God? When was the last time that happened?

Shifting a conversation to the spiritual category offers a particular form of connection and even healing, especially when it comes to conversations between people of different ethnicities and abilities. In the research on the habits of the mind needed to promote racial equity and inclusion, personal transformation, and interpersonal connection, James Longhurst and Juanita Brown discuss the needed shift from the material to the spiritual as "the pathway to human connection." They write, "We must see people at a different level. We must discover what lies underneath—their hopes, fears, dreams, regrets, and memories of joy, loss, and wonder. These experiences are what connect us all; we are linked together by these spiritual matters—matters of the heart . . . Gradually we realize that we are all connected as members of one family—the human family."[15] Seeing spiritual conversations as a curious exploration about another person means we are finding what connects us all through our spirits or souls.

IN ANY SITUATION

Now you have six pathways to enter into loving connection with others. In any situation, you can ask initial questions in any of the categories and then use any combination of questions to continue the conversation. Essentially, you can enjoy endless permutations and unlimited possibilities for every conversation. You'll never feel stuck again. You'll never wonder what to say or do next. Can you imagine your first conversation tomorrow? What will you ask? How will you follow up? Now imagine how your conversation tomorrow might leave you and your friend encouraged, growing, and marveling. Tomorrow, you will feel less alone. Tomorrow is a new day to love people—and allow them to love you—with better conversations.

PART THREE

A Daily Practice

CHAPTER NINE

DISCOVERING YOUR DEFAULT CONVERSATION

But we are all creatures of habit. It is far too easy to stay in the familiar ruts we dig for ourselves.

—Patrick Rothfuss, author

THROUGH THE PROCESS OF researching and writing this book, I've learned so much about myself, my friends, and the beautiful ways God made us. We have an extraordinary capacity for connection. Each of you reading this offers something beautiful, mysterious, and unique to any conversation. I like to read this quote to my students from psychologist Mary Pipher: "All of this individuality that is you, properly understood and clearly presented, is a tremendous gift to the world. It is a one-of-a-kind point of view on the universe."[1] You offer this tremendous gift to others as you ask questions and share your life in conversation. Yet, as I think about helping others grow in the art of conversation, I realize we can all think about expanding the categories for how we understand ourselves and relate to others. Unfortunately, I find myself and others stuck in conversational patterns based on what I call our "default conversations"—or the conversations we always tend to have out of habit, personality, or interest.

When you begin talking to other people, what question do you tend to ask first? I have a theory that the questions we like to ask others often relate to the area of our own lives we feel most comfortable about. Consider the list below and rank what happens in conversation. Where are you most likely to begin and continue in a conversation?

1. Do you ask about something physical? (What are you listening to? What are you drinking? Where did you get those great shoes? Did you change your hair?)

2. Do you go to the social? (Who were you with? What friends were there?)

3. Emotional? (How are you feeling? What emotions did that bring up?)

4. Cognitive? (What did you think about that? How are you making sense of that?)

5. Volitional? (What's your new goal? What choice do you have? What did you do?)

6. Spiritual? (What are you thinking about God?)

How do you begin to expand your capacity to connect with others deeply and warmly through each category? Let's work through a journaling activity together.

Take your lowest ranking categories (your bottom three) and brainstorm a list of questions you could ask in that category that you haven't asked someone before.

Then, start a conversation with yourself and answer the following question:

What question do I wish people would ask me? What do I like to talk about in this category?

Social: I wish people would ask me about _____

_____.

Physical: I wish people would ask me about _____

_____.

Emotional: I wish people would ask me how I feel about

_____.

Cognitive: I wish people would ask me what I'm thinking about

_____.

Volitional: I wish people would ask me about this goal or decision

_____.

Spiritual: I wish people would ask me about _____

_____.

As we think about questions you'd like to answer in these categories, it helps us understand how to move beyond our default conversational mode. Not everyone wants or needs to talk about what we want to talk about all the time, and it's important to realize we all have tendencies in conversation. You may tend to only talk about sports or cooking or gardening when there's an entire universe of questions to ask in five other categories of being human. I may tend to only ask about the mind when the person I'm with might want or need to talk about another category.

Your default conversational mode tells you so much about who you are, where you draw joy and meaning, and what you spend most of your time doing. What you tend to like to ask others about and talk about yourself indicates what you like to offer in conversation about your life.

If you pay attention to what you enjoy talking about, you can better discern where to invest time in certain relationships. I seek out friends who enjoy talking about their mind and their relationship with God. I seek out friends who set goals, talk about their choices, and regularly discuss their spiritual practices. I have a harder time connecting with people who enjoy only talking about the social, emotional, or physical sides of life, but if that person is in my life—through family, community, or work—I know I can branch out of my default conversational mode to connect with them.

When I ask students what question they wish I would ask them, I learn so much about them. I can quickly discern how much they love talking about their relationships, including their pets. But when students turn the question back to me and ask what I wish they would ask me, I often stammer and don't feel self-aware enough to answer the question. Do I really like people asking about obvious things like my writing (cognitive), my children (social), my goals (volitional), or my daily rituals (physical)? Do I only like people asking about spiritual topics? Do I really dislike talking about my emotions? *What do I really like to talk about?*

What do I really like to talk about? Answer that question for yourself.

It turns out, I love asking people cognitive questions. I like to know what people are thinking, and then I tend to move to spiritual topics. I wish people would say, "Dr. H, tell us what you've been thinking about lately." It feels like my love language when people ask what's been on my mind.

For our second journaling activity, have a conversation with yourself based on these prompts in each category:

How is my body doing?

What's happening in my social life?

What emotions have I been feeling?

What have I been thinking about?

What are my goals or decisions?

Where is God in this for me?

Then, use this chart to consider where you'd like to go next in the conversation in each category. What question would you personally like to answer? Why or why not? Which question do you not like answering? Why or why not?

SOCIAL – Has this been affecting your relationships?

EMOTIONAL – How does this make you feel emotionally?

PHYSICAL – What does that feel, taste, smell, hear, sound like?

COGNITIVE – How are you making sense of this?

VOLITIONAL – What will you do?

SPIRITUAL – Where is God in this for you?

What I love about this inventory is that it shines a light on what you most like to offer in conversation both about yourself and what you enjoy discussing with others. You can even tell your friends up front what you love talking about and why. You add value to a conversation because of your unique disposition and conversational expertise in one of the dimensions of being human. In the categories that you don't feel as confident (or that you have no desire for), you can attempt to grow in those areas to become a better conversationalist. I want to become better at asking my family members about their feelings, but I also know they like to talk to me about God. The next chapter will help you discern another person's default conversation and how to bless them most when talking to them.

CHAPTER TEN

DISCOVERING ANOTHER PERSON'S PREFERRED CONVERSATION

Come alive *(idiom):*
to become excited and filled with energy

THIS PAST YEAR, I WATCHED and then listened carefully as I asked questions to others in conversation. I watched for visible signs of energy (smile, eyes widening, hand gestures) and listened for signs of interest (quicker speech, more words, slightly higher pitch to the voice). I've been in the college classroom for over twenty years; I know how to read the interest in the room and stoke the fire of a conversation wherever I see embers glowing. When I see and hear interest in a line of questioning, I know to linger in that spot. I know to keep asking questions on this topic and in this particular category of conversation.

In marriage, the skill of discovering what a spouse actually wants to talk about serves as a form of love. You might not enjoy talking about what your conversation partner wants to talk about, but what if you chose to stay curious and bless them in this way? My husband loves woodworking and anything involving working with his hands. He likes to talk about physical processes and manual labor. As you already know, I love talking about God and intellectual things. Together, we bring opposite desires into a conversation. But both of us have learned how to bless one another and our friends in conversations the *other* person enjoys. My husband, Ashley, will ask about what I'm reading in the Bible, things I'm praying about, and what's happening in the classroom. I'll ask him about his house projects or work systems.

We sat around a bonfire on New Year's Eve 2021. A couple attended who have been on the front lines of COVID health care work since the beginning of the pandemic. As doctors, they had so much they needed to process with the rest of us who wanted to love them in conversation. Of course, my husband wanted to know all the technical details and the *physical processes* they experience on the COVID ward in the hospital. He asked a question in the physical category related to the ventilators and the rehabilitation of the body. They gave one-word, quiet answers. I, of course, asked about how they were making sense of all the loss and how God had met them (cognitive and spiritual categories). They again gave confused answers like "I really don't know. I don't know." I tried again.

"How are you feeling? How have you been doing with all the emotions of being with COVID patients?"

They both started to cry. They both began talking over each other to talk about the fear, the sadness, and the nightmares. They talked about the hopeless feelings, and what it felt like to be there when a person dies. They talked about what it feels like to help someone start to breathe and walk on their own. We just kept asking, "What did that feel like? What were your emotions?"

And they kept talking. I never got my conversation about God or their final intellectual conclusions about COVID. Ashley never got his conversation about the physical elements he was interested in. When we drove home that night, my husband remarked how important it is to follow the lead of what others need to talk about. We could have kept pushing our agenda—based on our default conversational modes—and missed an opportunity to deeply and warmly connect with our friends over their emotions.

We are both learning to listen and observe to discover what other people want and need to talk about. To start developing this skill of discovering another person's default or preferred conversation, try these techniques:

Listen and observe: Which questions elicit one-word answers with no facial expression or rise in speech volume? Which questions make people tilt their head in thought as if they want to consider their answer and enjoy giving it? Which questions make someone say, "Oh, that's a great question. I'm so glad you asked me that." Watch the facial expressions. Listen for the volume to rise. See if the person tilts their head, raises their eyebrows, or even leans forward (or changes position at all) to indicate increased interest.

Try questions and statements whose answers reveal their category of interest:

1. *Tell me the story about how . . .*

When the person answers that question, you'll gain immediate insight into what they want to talk about. For example, imagine your friend down the street just purchased a new car (or a boat or dog—anything). You say, "Hey! Tell me the story about that new car!"

Then listen to what they want to tell you. Will it be about the people involved (social)? Will they mention the way the car makes their body feel or the physical aspects of the car (physical)? Will they talk about what they were thinking about when they bought the car (cognitive)? Will they go right into their decision-making process (volitional)? Will they mention their emotions (emotional)? God (spiritual)? Try this with your friends, and you'll quickly discover what category of being human matters to them.

2. *Revise old stand-bys.*

Another question that helps reveal a person's favorite conversational category involves revising the cliché or ordinary go-to questions related to weather, sports, or even the overused question, "How are you?" Try these revisions to the common questions, and listen carefully to which category of being human the other person discusses with you:

> Instead of a weather question like, "Can you believe this weather?" ask this: "Are you a snow person?"

> Instead of "How are you?" (which inevitably produced the requisite response of "fine") ask, "What feels good today?"

> Instead of the sports question, "How 'bout that game, eh?" ask, "What are your game day rituals?"

I tried each of these revisions when I recently served as the Welcome Center and Information Desk host at our church. In this role, new visitors as well as church members spanning the generations stop by, lean over, and offer a greeting. It's impossible to not say anything since I'm one of the first people anyone sees and passes as they enter the sanctuary. This time, since I knew a big snowstorm was coming, I said, "What do you think about this big snow coming? Are you a snow person?"

What happened next fascinated me. Asking, "Are you a snow person?" invited a response with a justification or defense of the answer.

I loved the responses in all six categories of being human:

No! I hate the snow, but my grandchildren are coming to sled. Last time they came, we had the best time. We're going out before the storm to purchase more sleds! This led to a beautiful conversation about my own memories of sledding and the joy of childhood. This social category of conversation delighted both of us.

Yes! I love the snow! I'm going hiking later. Then I'll try some photography. This led to a conversation in both the physical and volitional category of where we enjoy hiking in Pennsylvania, how we take photographs, and why we both chose certain iPhones for the camera. I had never spoken to this person before, and within five minutes, we were connecting over snowflake photography and our choices for the day ahead.

Yes and no. Let me tell you about my dog-sitting business and how one dog won't go out in the snow. It's stressing me out! I have to bundle us both up in 6-degree weather and coax that dog to do his stuff. I'm nervous about today and the storm. This conversation in the emotional category involved us discussing the joys and sorrows of a pet-sitting business. We transitioned to a spiritual conversation about whether we might ask God to supernaturally help that dog overcome his fear of the snow.

Yes, but did you notice how every weather service predicts a different snowfall amount? I personally predict a dusting. I think . . . This led to a cognitive discussion of our theories of weather prediction.

Next week, I'll remember to ask these friends questions in the categories they most like to discuss and I'll follow up about that little dog who wouldn't go in the snow.

3. *Run down the list of the six conversational categories and see where your friends linger.*

My neighbor's son recently had knee surgery. When I stopped by to check on him and bring him some homemade cookies, I ran down the list of the six conversations to see if I could figure out what he would want to talk about. It went like this:

Hey! How are you feeling? *Fine.* (Nope—he doesn't want to talk about emotions.)

Was your girlfriend able to visit you during the surgery? *Yup. She came.* (Noted. He doesn't need to talk about social things.)

What made you decide you had to get the surgery? *Basketball injury.* (Still simple answers. No excitement about the volitional category.)

What's this making you think about your semester? *I don't know.* (Cognitive? Nope.)

Does it hurt? What's your physical therapy going to be like? *It doesn't really hurt. Isn't that amazing? They cut all into me, and it doesn't hurt. And I don't have to take the pain meds. I do have these exercises I have to do every day. I can show you. And the anesthesia was so weird!* (Bingo! He wants to talk about his body in the physical category!)

As you listen and observe, use some questions and statements to unearth categories of interests, or simply run down the list of the six conversational categories, you'll quickly discover a meaningful direction for your conversation that will bless your conversation partner.

CHAPTER ELEVEN

MOVING TOWARD THE GREATEST CONVERSATION

"Where are you?"
—Genesis 3:9

I'VE BEEN WONDERING SOMETHING as I conclude this book. I've been wondering if *the most important thing* we do as humans—and the thing that most reflects the generous, overflowing, sharing life of the triune God—is to *connect* with one another and ultimately, to God. Human conversation creates harmony between people and leads us to the joy of what the Bible calls communion or fellowship. This communion reflects something profound about God. Theologian Michael Reeves writes in *Delighting in the Trinity: An Introduction to the Christian Faith* about this harmony I so desire in my own life: "The Father, Son and Spirit have always been in delicious harmony, and thus they create a world where harmonies—distinct beings, persons or notes working in unity—are good, mirroring the very being of the triune God. The eternal harmony of the Father, Son and Spirit provides the logic for a world in which everything was created to exist in cheerful conviviality."[1]

Can you imagine a world of "cheerful conviviality," of rich fellowship and unity, and deep belonging? Can you imagine your own heart overflowing with love for your neighbor that you demonstrate in authentic conversation with a desire to know another person and invite them to know you? What if, wherever you are and wherever you go in your life, you decide to become a person *creating communion* with others, especially the overlooked, forgotten, or suffering person living near you right now?

Perhaps this is the godliest thing we do. Perhaps conversation most closely reflects the beauty and nature of God Himself.

When I decided to humble myself and learn from other people and welcome them into my own life as part of my journey—in my teaching, in my neighborhood, and even in my own family—the marvelous seed of communion took root and grew. Krista Tippett explains what happens to us in this choice to welcome others in:

> We have to be educated by the other. My heart cannot be educated by myself. It can only come out of a relationship with others. And if we accept being educated by others, to let them explain to us what happens to them, and to let yourself be immersed in their world so that they can get into our world, then you begin to share something very deep. You will never be the person in front of you, but you will have created what we call communion. I feel that this is the essence of life and that's what Jesus came to teach us.[2]

The "essence of life" Tippett describes—of sharing our lives with others—reflects something deeply theological and reflective of God Himself as relational and in fellowship as Father, Son, and Holy Spirit. The story of the entire Bible, then, involves a narrative of reconciliation of broken relationships; sin has estranged us from God, from ourselves, and from each other. This fracturing accounts for the existential loneliness and the wrongness we have felt or feel now. We don't know God. We don't know ourselves. We don't know others.

Knowing ourselves and who we are in relation to God gives us a starting point of where all great conversations flow. We let the love of God flow through us to others. We allow conversations to become sacred spaces where the Holy Spirit, in the words of Reeves, *vitalizes, refreshes,* and *makes fruitful* our words to one another.[3]

While this book primarily looks outward to conversation with others, we might use the strategies to build a deeper awareness of how we commune with God. We might listen to the questions God asks in the Bible and spend time thinking of prayer as a conversation with God—one in which He too believes the best about us, delights in how we share our lives with Him, and who, in turn, reveals more of Himself to us. Growing in our experience of God's attentiveness to us helps us reflect something divine in how we talk to ourselves and others.

GOD'S QUESTIONS TO US

I recently examined the questions Jesus asks in the New Testament that invite the kind of conversational goals mentioned in chapter 4. His questions inevitably lead to *encouragement, growth,* and *worship,* even if they initially convict or disturb others. His questions also span the gamut of human experience we've outlined in the six dimensions of being human. In the book of Matthew, you'll find that Jesus asks about our emotions (Why do you worry? Why are you afraid? Does this offend you? Why are you crying? Do you love Me?), our volition (What do you want? What do you want Me to do for you? Do you want to get well?), our thoughts (What do you think? Do you understand?), our social life (Did others talk to you about Me?), and our physical experiences (Do you have any fish? Do you see these great buildings?). *Jesus asks questions to engage people in meaningful*

*conversation—often to draw them out deeper into fellowship with Him-
self and others. God's questions have always been aimed to bring people
out of hiding and into sacred spaces of truth.*

If we remember from Genesis 3, after the serpent deceives Eve
and she eats the forbidden fruit, both Adam and Eve *go into hiding*.
We read this:

> And they heard the sound of the LORD God walking in the garden
> in the cool of the day, and the man and his wife hid themselves
> from the presence of the LORD God among the trees of the gar-
> den. But the LORD God called to the man and said to him, "Where
> are you?" And he said, "I heard the sound of you in the garden,
> and I was afraid, because I was naked, and I hid myself." He said,
> "Who told you that you were naked? Have you eaten of the tree of
> which I commanded you not to eat?" The man said, "The woman
> whom you gave to be with me, she gave me fruit of the tree, and
> I ate." Then the LORD God said to the woman, "What is this that
> you have done?" The woman said, "The serpent deceived me, and
> I ate." (Gen. 3:8–13)

Did you notice God's questions?

Where are you?

Who told you that you were naked?

What is this that you have done?

These conversational questions reveal something special about
God in our own lives today. I imagine God asking us right now itera-
tions of these ancient questions in the garden. *Where are we in relation
to Him? Is anything hidden? Is God dwelling within us? Where are we?*
Imagine God asking you, "Where are you? I've been looking for you!"

Next, the question "Who told you. . . ?" makes me think about who

I'm listening to in the culture. *To whom do we run for truth? What is our current source of wisdom? Who are we authorizing to tell us about ourselves?* Imagine God asking you, "Who is telling you all this stuff about yourself? Who are you listening to besides Me?"

Finally, the volitional question comes. "What have you done?" invites the kind of analysis that leads us to repentance. It reminds us that we make choices every day—even in our attitudes and thoughts—that fall short of God's commands. We do not obey, and we find, even in our best efforts to be good, that we fail. But rather than the curse that comes next in Genesis, we find Jesus, who takes the curse for us so we can come out of hiding (Gal. 3:13). We find a God who not only asks where we are, but who leaves everyone behind to seek after us like that one lost sheep (Luke 15). We find Jesus, who stands as our Advocate against the accuser, Satan, who accuses us night and day (Rev. 12:10). And we find Jesus forgives our sin and cleanses us from all unrighteousness (1 John 1:9). *Where are you? Who told you that? What have you done?* Every person must answer these questions in their own conversation with God, who asks us questions to lead us to truth and abundant life in Him.

As we let a resurrected Christ live through us by the Holy Spirit, our questions to others reflect His heart to seek and save the lost (Where are you?), to help others arrive at truth (Who told you that?), and to help people come out of hiding from shame and guilt (What have you done?), because they have a forgiveness of sins and right standing before God and others. Genesis 3 resonates deeply with another conversation we read in Scripture, but this time, it's with a different woman who also lives in hiding. She's a Samaritan—outcast and alone—who has come to the well to draw water.

Jesus begins a conversation with an outcast, and if you read John 4:7–26 in tandem with Genesis 3, you'll see how a similar conversation unfolds in light of Christ's redeeming love for us.

A woman from Samaria came to draw water. Jesus said to her, "Give me a drink." (For his disciples had gone away into the city to buy food.) The Samaritan woman said to him, "How is it that you, a Jew, ask for a drink from me, a woman of Samaria?" (For Jews have no dealings with Samaritans.) Jesus answered her, "If you knew the gift of God, and who it is that is saying to you, 'Give me a drink,' you would have asked him, and he would have given you living water." The woman said to him, "Sir, you have nothing to draw water with, and the well is deep. Where do you get that living water? Are you greater than our father Jacob? He gave us the well and drank from it himself, as did his sons and his live-stock." Jesus said to her, "Everyone who drinks of this water will be thirsty again, but whoever drinks of the water that I will give him will never be thirsty again. The water that I will give him will become in him a spring of water welling up to eternal life." The woman said to him, "Sir, give me this water, so that I will not be thirsty or have to come here to draw water."

Jesus said to her, "Go, call your husband, and come here." The woman answered him, "I have no husband." Jesus said to her, "You are right in saying, 'I have no husband'; for you have had five hus-bands, and the one you now have is not your husband. What you have said is true." The woman said to him, "Sir, I perceive that you are a prophet. Our fathers worshiped on this mountain, but you say that in Jerusalem is the place where people ought to worship." Jesus said to her, "Woman, believe me, the hour is coming when nei-ther on this mountain nor in Jerusalem will you worship the Fa-ther. You worship what you do not know; we worship what we know, for salvation is from the Jews. But the hour is coming, and is now here, when the true worshipers will worship the Father in spirit and truth, for the Father is seeking such people to worship him. God is spirit, and those who worship him must worship in spirit and truth." The woman said to him, "I know that Messiah is coming (he who is called Christ). When he comes, he will tell us all things." Jesus said to her, "I who speak to you am he."

We observe several fascinating similarities between Eve and the Samaritan woman. Both women are called out of a form of hiding (the Samaritan is an outcast who must draw from the well alone, outside of community). Both women must deal with eating or drinking, and what's allowed or not. Both women must reckon with the condemning truth about life choices (the Samaritan woman has had six lovers). Both women must think about where their source of truth comes from. But this time, instead of enduring a curse, the woman in the presence of Jesus gains knowledge of a Savior who then gives her a great ministry in Samaria where many "from that town believed in [Jesus] because of the woman's testimony" (John 4:39). She is offered living water and rich communion with the same voice of invitation we shall all hear where God says, "'Come.' And let the one who is thirsty come; let the one who desires take the water of life without price" (Rev. 22:17).

When Jesus initiates a conversation, we find the same questions at play from Genesis 3: *Where are you? Who told you this information? What have you done?* Now, however, we come out of hiding. We don't experience condemnation. We instead gain only truth and intimacy with our Savior.

OUR QUESTIONS TO GOD

Maybe it's time we all started having better conversations with God. When we talk to God in prayer, we can approach this like a real conversation with real dialogue because God speaks through His Word and through the Holy Spirit, animating His Word to our unique situation.

I talk to God throughout the day, but generally, my best conversations with God happen between 6:30–7:30 a.m. every morning of my life. I sit in my mustard recliner and gaze out at the weeping cherry tree in my front yard as the sun rises. I keep my Bible and a journal on a table beside me to record questions I ask God and how He answers. This morning routine involves a cup of coffee, a warm blanket, and usually, my cat, Snowflake, curled up beside me.

My conversations with God mirror my best conversations with others in that I adopt the Four Mindsets and the Three Fresh Goals of Conversation. I believe the absolute best I can of God. I think of how He cannot help but bless because it's in His nature to do so. I praise Him as Creator and Wonderful Counselor. I tell Him all the good things I'm thinking about Him. I stay curious about Him and what He's doing in the world and how He works in our lives. I'm invested in His mission to seek and save the lost. And I'm committed to sharing everything with Him. It's the best friendship I have and ever will have.

And I do ask Him questions. Most recently, I asked God a desperate question. I sat on a Monday morning during the bitter winter, and I cried over the tragic loss of my dear friend's son. The grief felt overwhelming, but I nevertheless had to start a new January semester at Penn State. What would normally be a joyful and lighthearted first day of class now felt impossible for me as I sat under the heavy weight of sorrow. So I asked God my question:

How can I go to work when I am also grieving?

I waited to see if the Holy Spirit would bring to mind anything from Scripture that could help me. Curiously, I had been reading the book of Matthew chapter by chapter, and I suddenly remembered something about Jesus. I quickly flipped to Matthew 14. What unfolded next astonished and then delighted me. In Matthew 14, Jesus is also grieving the loss of someone special. John the Baptist has just been beheaded, and Jesus has retreated all by Himself, presumably to grieve. But there's no time to grieve; Jesus also must go to work. I smiled when I saw the comparison to my own situation. I had a crowd of students waiting for me on campus, just like Jesus had a crowd waiting for Him. We read this:

> Now when Jesus heard this, he withdrew from there in a boat to a desolate place by himself. But when the crowds heard it, they followed him on foot from the towns. When he went ashore he saw a great crowd, and he had compassion on them and healed their sick. Now when it was evening, the disciples came to him and said, "This is a desolate place, and the day is now over; send the crowds away to go into the villages and buy food for themselves." But Jesus said, "They need not go away; you give them something to eat." They said to him, "We have only five loaves here and two fish." And he said, "Bring them here to me." Then he ordered the crowds to sit down on the grass, and taking the five loaves and the two fish, he looked up to heaven and said a blessing. Then he broke the loaves and gave them to the disciples, and the disciples gave them to the crowds. And they all ate and were satisfied. And they took up twelve baskets full of the broken pieces left over. And those who ate were about five thousand men, besides women and children. (vv. 13–21)

I wanted to send my students away—perhaps cancel class or move to an online discussion for the day—but I noted Jesus' compassion. I noted how He asked what resources the disciples had so they could feed this crowd. *Five loaves. Two fish. Impossible.* I kept reading. When Jesus gets ahold of those limited resources, He performs a miracle of provision. I underlined how "they all ate and were satisfied."

I said to the Lord: "You know I have a crowd to teach. You know I have nothing emotionally to offer and my brain feels like it's in a fog. Lord, can You take the limited resources I have and multiply them? Can you make my classes so good today that everyone will be 'satisfied' like in this miracle?"

I felt empowered as I left my house to teach with my intellectual and emotional resources that felt like five loaves and two fish. I trusted God to bring laughter and community to my classes that day, and He did! All afternoon, I thanked Him for being a God that provides and how Jesus understood exactly what it felt like to be grieving and also needing to work. It felt like a special day with the Lord.

But the miracle didn't stop for me there. As I stood in the kitchen that evening, my husband said, "Who ordered two cases of KN95 masks? We have two enormous boxes on our doorstep!"

"I did order KN95 masks, but just two small boxes," I insisted. "And these masks aren't cheap!"

"Well, the company sent *cases*, not boxes. What do we do? They only charged us for the two little boxes." We started laughing nervously as we realized our two small boxes multiplied to 1,500 masks due to a shipping error. After contacting the company and explaining the confusion, the company apologized for the mistake but then told us not to bother shipping them back. We could freely distribute the masks without cost to whoever needed them.

I paid for two small boxes—just like a boy holding up two little fish—and here I had my own object lesson of the day's provision (which my daughter likes to remind me is nearly 5,000 masks since you can wear a single KN95 anywhere from three to five times). We loved contacting all the thankful neighbors who were having troubling finding good masks, and I had a chance to tell the neighbors my story from the morning of Matthew 14. What was so stunning for us involved how, even a week later after distributing all the masks to any family who wanted a box or two, we still had twelve boxes left over just like in the biblical account.

It was as if God was telling me—through Matthew 14, through my teaching, and through the example of those boxes that became cases—that yes, He heard my question and had an answer I could hear throughout the day: we give God our weakness, and He turns it to strength to bless the crowd. He meets us in our pain. He teaches us from His Word. He answers our questions. He is a God of beautiful and loving conversation with us.

AND NOW OTHERS

Conversations with God refuel us for the journey of offering meaningful connection with others. We draw from the deep well of His love, joy, and hope to encourage others, help them grow, and usher their souls into awe. We know God's grace powerfully, so we choose to believe the best about others. We stand humbled and marveling before the mystery of other people and we live in stunning curiosity about them. We yoke our lives to theirs in communion. And we share our lives generously, fearlessly, and authentically.

When we engage in meaningful conversation with others, we enter into a *sacred space*. If we allow it to, a conversation becomes holy ground. No conversation is an accident or without a divine purpose. There's always something to ask about others—whether social, physical, emotional, cognitive, volitional, or spiritual. And we can use those questions to encourage, help one another grow, and ultimately lead us to worship. As you put this book down and encounter another person, you have everything you need for warm, loving connection.

I wish I could sit with you and join this great conversation. You have so much to offer of yourself. Are you as excited as I am? What will you ask next?

APPENDIX

PROFESSOR HOLLEMAN'S 100 FAVORITE QUESTIONS TO GET TO KNOW HER STUDENTS (OR ANYONE)

1. What is the most interesting course you have ever taken in school?

2. What is your favorite quotation?

3. What is one item you might keep forever?

4. What were you known for in high school? Did you have any nicknames?

5. If you could have witnessed any event in sports history, what would it be?

6. What is something you consider beautiful?

7. What was your first song you played over and over again?

8. What accomplishment are you most proud of?

9. If you could be an apprentice to any person, from whom would you want to learn?

10. What are three things that make you happy?

11. What's one movie you think everyone should see? What's a movie nobody should see?

12. Who inspires you?

13. What's one thing you want to do before you die?

14. Get in groups of three people. What's the most bizarre thing you have in common?

15. Whenever you are having a bad day, what is the best thing you can do to cheer yourself up?

16. Have you ever experienced something unexplainable or supernatural?

17. What was your best Halloween costume?

18. What's the last item you purchased and why?

19. What was the last thing you Googled out of pure curiosity?

20. What YouTube or TikTok video do you watch over and over?

21. What's the kindest act you've ever witnessed?

22. Tell us one thing you know you do well (a talent?) and one thing you know you cannot do.

23. What is your favorite way to procrastinate?

24. What is your favorite home-cooked meal?

25. What was your favorite childhood toy?

26. What clubs are you involved in?

27. What was your first paid job?

28. Have you met a famous person? Who?

29. What's the story behind your name?

30. Do you believe in anything that most people might not believe in?

31. How would you answer this: I wish everyone would

_____.

32. What's the best sound effect you can make?

33. What's the funniest thing you did as a kid that people still talk about today?

34. What idea do you think is worth arguing about?

35. What is something quirky about you?

36. For what reason do others often seek your help or input?

37. What is your guilty pleasure—something you love that almost embarrasses you?

38. What is one thing that's important for others to know about you?

39. Do you still do anything today that you also loved to do as a child?

40. Do you have any daily rituals?

41. What is the most misunderstood word you can think of?

42. What is the first book you remember changing you somehow?

43. What piece of wisdom do you like to pass on?

44. Do you have an irrational fear or strange addiction?

45. What's been the most surprising thing about this stage of life you're in now?

46. What is your biggest pet peeve?

47. Who are your animal friends?

48. What's your latest failure?

49. What's something new you've learned this week?

50. What thought keeps you up at night?

51. What's a question you like people to ask you?

52. What's one thing that truly fascinates you?

53. Think of the best community you've been a part of. What made this community so great?

54. If you had to pick a song for your "entrance music," what would it be?

55. What's something funny or surprising that happened to you lately?

56. When did you do something you thought you couldn't do this year? When were you brave?

57. What are you learning?

58. What is your latest victory in life?

59. When was the last time you felt really good about yourself? What was happening?

60. Tell us about an encounter you had with a stranger, a strange place, or a strange animal.

61. What's something that made you experience wonder or awe this year?

62. What's something you experienced in childhood that children today don't experience?

63. What's one piece of good news?

64. What's stressing you out most today?

65. What changes when you enter a room?

66. If you had to sing a karaoke song, which one would you choose?

67. What could be the best compliment someone could give you?

68. What trait do you most admire in someone else?

69. How would you want others to describe you?

70. What do you look forward to each day?

71. What is the most heartwarming thing you've ever seen?

72. What have you most recently formed an opinion about?

73. Where is the most relaxing place you've ever been?

74. What fictional place would you most like to go to?

75. What are you most likely to become famous for?

76. What's worth spending more on to get the best?

77. What is special about the place you grew up?

78. What fad or trend do you hope comes back?

79. Where's the farthest you've ever been from home?

80. What takes up too much of your time?

81. What's an essential workplace item for you?

82. What job would you be terrible at?

83. What's the story behind the longest you've ever gone without sleep?

84. How is your day going on a scale of 1 to 10? What would make it a 10?

85. What do you like to do the old-fashioned way?

86. What popular TV or movie do you refuse to watch?

87. What's the story behind a piece of clothing or jewelry you're wearing?

88. What concept do you try to explain but often feel misunderstood when you do?

89. What is your ideal city to live in and why?

90. Have you ever tried to grow something? What happened?

91. What's overrated? What's underrated?

92. What's something you didn't want to do but were glad you did?

93. What's your signature meal? What's the best meal you've ever had?

94. What are your tips for staying hydrated?

95. What's your favorite study spot?

96. What is your role in a group or in your family?

97. What feels like "home" to you?

98. How do you pass the time on an airplane/train/car trip?

99. What did you bring for show-and-tell as a child? If you can't remember, what would you bring for show-and-tell now?

100. What quality do you most respect in other people and why?

ACKNOWLEDGMENTS

MY HIGHEST GRATITUDE goes to Ashley Holleman, who formed the concept of the six conversations and helped me think through the best ways to help others connect meaningfully. Darrell and Stephanie Velegol cheered me on in countless ways from the day we reconnected as neighbors due to the COVID lockdown. As always, my colleagues at Penn State and beyond, especially Mary Sellers, Gigi McNamara, Kimi Grant, JoAnn and Erik Foley-DeFiore, and Faith McDonald, offered life-giving conversation as I wrote this book. I continue to treasure my friends, neighbors, students, and family (who let me try out my conversation questions on them—especially the Kish family and my daughters, Sarah and Kate!). Thank you to Sandy Mackin for our awe walks and for her prayers as I wrote this book. Special thanks to Tawny Johnson at Illuminate Literary Agency for her wisdom and direction. Most importantly, thank you to the team at Moody Publishers, including Judy Dunagan and Pam Pugh, who bring my books to life.

NOTES

Introduction: A Conversation Revival

1. "The Happiness Effect," *Bulletin of the World Health Organization*, 89 (2011): 246–47, https://doi.org/10.2471/BLT.11.020411.

2. Emily Boudreau, "Combatting an Epidemic of Loneliness," *Harvard Graduate School of Education*, February 9, 2021, https://www.gse.harvard.edu/news/21/02/combatting-epidemic-loneliness.

3. "Cigna Study Reveals Loneliness at Epidemic Levels in America," *Cigna Newsroom*, May 1, 2018, https://www.cigna.com/about-us/newsroom/news-and-views/press-releases/2018 new-cigna-study-reveals-loneliness-at-epidemic-levels-in-america.

4. Rick Noack, "Isolation Is Rising in Europe. Can Loneliness Ministers Help Change That?" *Washington Post,* February 2, 2018, https://www.washington post.com/news/worldviews/wp/2018/02/02/isolation-is-rising-in-europe-can-loneliness-ministers-help-change-that/.

5. Katie Warren, "Japan Has Appointed a 'Minister of Loneliness' After Seeing Suicide Rates in the Country Increase for the First Time in 11 Years," *Insider*, February 22, 2021, https://www.insider.com/japan-minister-of-loneliness-suicides-rise-pandemic-2021-2.

6. Matthew Solovey, "Four Themes Identified as Contributors to Diseases of Despair in Pennsylvania," *Penn State Research New*s, July 23, 2021, https://www.psu.edu/news/research/story/four-themes-identified-contributors-diseases-despair-pennsylvania/.

Chapter One: The Four Mindsets of a Loving Conversation

1. Julien C. Mirivel, *The Art of Positive Communication: Theory and Practice* (New York: Peter Lang, International Academic Publishers, 2014), 7.

2. J. A. Hess, A. D. Fannin, and L. H. Pollom, "Creating Closeness: Discerning and Measuring Strategies for Fostering Closer Relationships," *Personal Relationships*, 14 (2007): 25–44.

3. Dale Carnegie, *How to Win Friends and Influence People* (New York: Simon and Schuster, 1998), 52.

4. Eugene Beresin, MD, "Why Are Teens So Lonely, and What Can They Do About It?" *Psychology Today*, July 26, 2019, https://www.psychologytoday.com/us/blog/inside-out-outside-in/201907/why-are-teens-so-lonely-and-what-can-they-do-about-it.

5. Todd Kashdan, quoted in Jill Suttie, "Why Curious People Have Better Relationships," *Greater Good Magazine: Science-Based Insights for a Meaningful Life*, May 31, 2017, https://greatergood.berkeley.edu/article/item/why_curious_people_have_better_relationships.

6. Todd Kashdan, quoted in Markham Heid, "Curiosity Is the Secret to a Happy Life," *Elemental*, February 13, 2020, https://elemental.medium.com/curiosity-is-the-secret-to-a-happy-life-3dc5d940d602.

7. Susan Sprecher, "Creating Closeness and Interdependence: Results of Laboratory-Based Studies Involving Getting-Acquainted Dyads," in *Interdependence, Interaction, and Close Relationships*, eds. Laura V. Machia, Christopher R. Agnew, and Ximena B. Arriaga (Cambridge: Cambridge University Press, 2020), 343–67.

8. Todd B. Kashdan et al., "The Five-Dimensional Curiosity Scale: Capturing the Bandwidth of Curiosity and Identifying Four Unique Subgroups of Curious People," *Journal of Research in Personality* 73 (2018): 130–49.

9. Mary Pipher, *Writing to Change the World: An Inspiring Guide for Transforming the World with Words* (New York: Penguin, 2006), 45–46.

10. Todd Kashdan and M. F. Steger, "Curiosity and Pathways to Well-Being and Meaning in Life: Traits, States, and Everyday Behaviors," *Motivation and Emotion* 31 (2007): 159–73, https://doi.org/10.1007/s11031-007-9068-7.

11. Jill Suttie, "Why Curious People Have Better Relationships," *Greater Good Magazine: Science-Based Insights for a Meaningful Life*, May 31, 2017, https://greatergood.berkeley.edu/article/item/why_curious_people_have_better_relationships.

12. Roger Schwarz, "Being Genuinely Curious," Roger Schwarz & Associates, May 2005, http://www.schwarzassociates.com/managing-performance/being-genuinely-curious/.

13. Mandy Len Catron, "To Fall in Love with Anyone, Do This," *New York Times*, January 9, 2015, https://www.nytimes.com/2015/01/11/style/modern-love-to-fall-in-love-with-anyone-do-this.html.

14. Arthur Aron et al., "The Experimental Generation of Interpersonal Closeness: A Procedure and Some Preliminary Findings," *Personality and Social Psychology Bulletin* (1997): 363–77, doi:10.1177/0146167297234003.

15. Daniel Jones, "The 36 Questions That Lead to Love," *New York Times*, January 9, 2016, https://www.nytimes.com/2015/01/09/style/no-37-big-wedding-or-small.html.

16. Mary Pipher, *Writing to Change the World*, 45–46.

17. As quoted in ibid., 93.

18. Lauren Kelly McHenry, "A Qualitative Exploration of Unconditional Positive Regard and Its Opposite Constructs in Coach-Athlete Relationships" (Master's Thesis, University of Tennessee, 2018), https://trace.tennessee.edu/utk_gradthes/5046.

19. Evi Makri-Botsari, "Adolescents' Unconditional Acceptance by Parents and Teachers and Educational Outcomes: A Structural Model of Gender Differences," *Journal of Adolescence* 43 (August 2015): 50–62.

20. Natalie Schefer, Abraham Carmeli, and Ravit Cohen-Meitar, "Bringing Carl Rogers Back In: Exploring the Power of Positive Regard at Work," *British Journal of Management* 29 (November 2017): 63–81.

21. Josh Packard and Ellen Koneck, *Belonging: Reconnecting America's Loneliest Generation* (Denver: Springtide Research Institute 2020), 68, 7.

22. Nathaniel M. Lambert et al., "Benefits of Expressing Gratitude to a Partner Changes One's View of the Relationship," *Psychological Science* (March 5, 2010): 1–7, https://doi.org/10.1177%2F0956797610364003.

23. Abdulati Ahmed, "Transforming Relationships Through Positive Communication," *Online Journal of the Faculty of Communication Sciences* 27 (2019): 206–19, retrieved from https://dergipark.org.tr/en/pub/kurgu/issue/59730/861424.

24. M. S. Clark, L. A. Beck, and O. R. Aragón, "Relationship Initiation: Bridging the Gap Between Initial Attraction and Well-Functioning Communal Relationships," in B. H. Fiese, M. Celano, K. Deater-Deckard, E. N. Jouriles, and M. A. Whisman (eds.), *APA Handbooks in Psychology®. APA Handbook of Contemporary Family Psychology: Foundations, Methods, and Contemporary Issues Across the Lifespan*, American Psychological Association (2019): 409–25, https://doi.org/10.1037/0000099-023.

25. Julien Mirivel, *The Art of Positive Communication: Theory and Practice* (New York: Peter Lang, 2014), 8.

26. Hess et al., "Creating Closeness," 29.

27. Ibid., 25–44.

Chapter Two: A Theology of a Loving Conversation

1. Crossway Bibles, *ESV Study Bible, English Standard Version* (Wheaton, IL: Crossway Bibles, 2008): 2275–76.

2. C. R. Agnew et al., "Cognitive Interdependence: Commitment and the Mental Representation of Close Relationships," *Journal of Personality and Social Psychology* (1998): 939–54, https://doi.org/10.1037/0022-3514.74.4.939.

3. See Arthur Aron et al., "Close Relationships as Including Other in the Self," *Journal of Personality and Social Psychology* (1991): 241–53, and Aron and C. Norman's chapter, "Self-expansion Model of Motivation and Cognition in Close Relationships and Beyond," in G. J. O. Fletcher and M. S. Clark (eds.), *Blackwell Handbook of Social Psychology* (Oxford, England: Blackwell, 2002): 478–501.

4. Sarah Ketay and Lindsey Beck, "Seeing You in Me: Preliminary Evidence for Perceptual Overlap Between Self and Close Others," *Journal of Social and Personal Relationships*, vol. 36 (July 24, 2018): 2474–86.

5. Eli J. Finkel, Jeffry A. Simpson, and Paul W. Eastwick, "The Psychology of Close Relationships: Fourteen Core Principles," *Annual Review of Psychology*, vol. 68 (January 3, 2017): 383–411.

6. C. S. Lewis, *The Four Loves* (United Kingdom: Harcourt Brace Jovnovich, 1991), 78.

Chapter Three: Our Current Climate

1. "The Brain's Reactive and Responsive Mode with Dr. Rick Hanson," video, October 19, 2017, https://www.youtube.com/watch?v=_SXQcBaITfY.

2. Debbie Hampton, "How to Change Your Brain from Reactive to Responsive," *The Best Brain Possible: Information and Inspiration for Anyone with a Brain*, September 4, 2016, https://thebestbrainpossible.com/how-to-change-your-brain-from-reactive-to-responsive/.

3. Nicole F. Roberts, "Your Brain on Drama: What Social Media Means for Your Personal Growth," *Forbes*, August 10, 2018, https://www.forbes.com/sites/nicolefisher/2018/08/10/your-brain-on-drama-what-your-social-media-means-for-personal-growth/?sh=104c3b187e9.

4. Ruth Tam interviews Tufts University professors Sarah Sobieraj and Jeffrey M. Berry about their book *The Outrage Industry: Public Opinion Media and the New Incivility* in "Wrath of the Talking Heads: How the 'Outrage Industry' Affects Politics," PSB News Hour, Febuary 28, 2014, https://www.pbs.org/newshour/politics/how-outrage-industry-affects-politics.

5. Ibid.

6. Ibid.

7. Ibid.

Chapter Four: What's a Conversation For?

1. Edmund Burke, *A Philosophical Enquiry into the Origin of our Ideas of the Sublime and Beautiful*, 2nd ed. (London: R. and J. Dodsley, 1759).

2. Edward Bonner and Harris L. Friedman, "A Conceptual Clarification of the Experience of Awe: An Interpretative Phenomenological Analysis," *The Humanistic Psychologist* 39, no. 3 (July 2011): 222–35.

3. Ibid.

4. Kirk Schneider, "The Resurgence of Awe in Psychology: Promise, Hope, and Perils," *The Humanistic Psychologist,* 45 (2017): 103–8, http://dx.doi.org/10.1037/hum0000060.

5. Y. Bai et al., "Awe, the Diminished Self, and Collective Engagement: Universals and Cultural Variations in the Small Self," *Journal of Personality and Social Psychology,* 113 (2017): 185–209, http://dx.doi.org/10.1037/pspa0000087.

6. Jennifer Stellar et al., "Self-Transcendent Emotions and Their Social Functions: Compassion, Gratitude, and Awe Bind Us to Others through Prosociality," *Emotion Review* 9, no. 3 (July 2017): 200–207, https://doi:10.1177/17540739-16684557.

7. Paul K. Piff et al., "Awe, the Small Self, and Prosocial Behavior," *Journal of Personality and Social Psychology* 108 (2015): 883–99, https://dx.doi.org/10.1037/pspi0000018.

8. V. E. Sturm et al., "Big Smile, Small Self: Awe Walks Promote Prosocial Positive Emotions in Older Adults," *Emotion* (2020): 1–16, https://dx.doi.org/10.1037/emo0000876.

9. Ibid., 1.

10. Ibid., 2.

11. Ibid.

12. Andy Tix, "7 Ways to Be Awe-Inspired in Everyday Life," *Psychology Today*, November 1, 2016, https://www.psychologytoday.com/us/blog/the-pursuit-peace/201611/7-ways-be-awe-inspired-in-everyday-life.

13. Ibid.

Chapter Five: What Goes Wrong in Conversation

1. Natalie Berry summarizes the research on positive mood in "Are Happy Students Successful Students?," *Science of Education* (February 17, 2013), https://natberryblog.wordpress.com/2013/02/17/are-happy-students-successful-students/.

2. Garson O'Toole, "Great Minds Discuss Ideas; Average Minds Discuss Events; Small Minds Discuss People," *Quote Investigator*, https://quoteinvestigator

.com/2014/11/18/great-minds/#:~:text=preoccupied%20with%20gossip%3A-,
Great%20minds%20discuss%20ideas%3B%20average%20minds%20discuss%
20events%3B%20small%20minds,find%20a%20solid%20supporting%20
citation.

3. Valerie Tiberius and John D. Walker, "Arrogance," *American Philosophical Quarterly* 35, no. 4 (October 1998): 379–90.

Chapter Six: Revisiting the Basics

1. Margaret Wheatley, *Turning to One Another: Simple Conversations to Restore Hope to the Future* (San Francisco: Berrett-Koehler Publishers, 2009), 38.

2. Ibid., 40.

3. Kory Floyd, "Empathic Listening as an Expression of Interpersonal Affection," *International Journal of Listening* 28 (January 8, 2014): 1–12, http://www.doi.org /10.1080/10904018.2014.861293.

4. W. R. Zakahi and B. Goss, "Loneliness and Interpersonal Decoding Skills," *Communication Quarterly* 43 (1995): 75–85, https://doi.org/10.1080/01463379-509369957.

5. Tim Irwin, *Extraordinary Influence: How Great Leaders Bring Out the Best in Others* (Hoboken, NJ: John Wiley and Sons, 2018), 59.

6. Eli Finkel, Jeffry Simpson, and Paul Eastwick, "The Psychology of Close Relationships: Fourteen Core Principles," *Annual Review of Psychology*, 68 (2017): 383–411.

7. Mordechai Gordon, "Listening as Embracing the Other: Martin Buber's Philosophy of Dialogue," *Educational Theory* 61 (June 20, 2011): 207–9, https:// doi.org/10.1111/j.1741-5446.2011.00400.x.

8. B. Thornton et al., "The Mere Presence of a Cell Phone May Be Distracting: Implications for Attention and Task Performance." *Social Psychology* 45 (2014): 479–88, https://doi.org/10.1027/1864-9335/a000216.

9. Dafna Lender, "Tuning into Attunement," *Psychotherapy Networker* (January 2018), 34.

10. Ibid.

Chapter Seven: Handling Fear and Self-Consciousness

1. C. S. Lewis, *The Four Loves* (San Diego: Harcourt Brace Jovanovich, 1991), 65.

2. Katherine R. Thorson et al., "Self-Disclosure is Associated with Adrenocortical Attunement Between New Acquaintances," *Psychoneuroendrocrinology* 132 (October 2021): 1–8.

3. Erica J. Boothby et al., "The Liking Gap in Conversations: Do People Like Us More Than We Think?" *Psychological Science* (2018): 1742, www.psychological science.org/PS.

4. Ibid., 1743.

5. Ibid., 1744.

6. Ibid., 1745.

7. Ibid., 1754.

8. Margaret Wheatley, *Turning to One Another: Simple Conversations to Restore Hope to the Future* (San Francisco: Berrett-Koehler Publishers, 2009), 28.

9. Eliza Bisbee Duffey, *The Ladies' and Gentleman's Etiquette: A Complete Manual of the Manners and Dress of American Society* (Philadelphia: Porter and Coates, 1877), 46.

10. Einav Hart, Eric M. VanEpps, and Maurice E. Schweitzer, "The (Better Than Expected) Consequences of Asking Sensitive Questions," *Organizational Behavior and Human Decision Processes* 162 (January 2021):136–54.

11. Todd Kashdan, quoted in Markham Heid, "Curiosity Is the Secret to a Happy Life," *Elemental,* February 13, 2020, https://elemental.medium.com/curiosity-is-the-secret-to-a-happy-life-3dc5d940d602.

12. I write about my teaching philosophy in a chapter called "Go Early" in *A Grander Story: An Invitation to Christian Professors* (Orlando: Cru Press, 2017), 145–56.

Chapter Eight: The Six Conversations

1. Mary Jo Asmus, "The Neuroscience of Asking Insightful Questions," *Government Executive,* April 26, 2017, https://www.govexec.com/management/2017/04/neuroscience-asking-insightful-questions/137274/.

2. David Hoffeld, "Want to Know What Your Brain Does When It Hears a Question?," *Fast Company,* February 21, 2017, https://www.fastcompany.com/3068341/want-to-know-what-your-brain-does-when-it-hears-a-question.

3. Margaret Wheatley in Juanita Brown et al., *The World Café: Shaping Our Futures Through Conversations That Matter* (San Francisco: Berrett-Koehler Publishers, Incorporated, 2005), *ProQuest Ebook Central*, https://ebookcentral.proquest.com/lib/pensu/detail.action?docID=483738.

4. Jeff Haden, "Forget Small Talk: Why Emotionally Intelligent People Embrace the Rule of the Awkward Conversation, Backed by Science," Apple News, *Inc.,* November 22, 2021.

5. Ibid.

6. Vanessa Van Edwards, "How to Have and Hold Dazzling Conversation with Anyone: We Review 11 Science Backed Steps," *Science of People,* https://www.scienceofpeople.com/have-hold-conversation/.

7. Email from Carla Panzellaa, PhD, Dean of Students, on Nov. 19, 2021.

8. Vanessa Van Edwards, "Jerry Seinfeld's Conversation Hack," https://www.youtube.com/watch?v=BExVtFFyEgw, accessed Jan. 3, 2022.

9. Joe Keohane, "How to Become a Master at Talking to Strangers," updated December 27, 2021, *Entrepreneur,* July 2021.

10. Ibid.

11. Ibid.

12. Krista Tippett, *Becoming Wise: An Inquiry into the Mystery and Art of Living* (New York: Penguin Press, 2016), 75.

13. Patrick Haggard, "Human Volition: Towards a Neuroscience of Will," *Nature Reviews Neuroscience* 9 (December 2008): 934–46, https://doi-org.ezaccess.libraries.psu.edu/10.1038/nrn2497.

14. As a Penn State professor, I know where to direct students to resources if they are in distress. You can always call the National Suicide Prevention Lifeline at 988 (for more information, visit 988lifeline.org) or the Domestic Violence Support (for more information, visit www.thehotline.org).

15. James Longhurst and Juanita Brown, "The Five Shifts: Ensuring an Environment for Healing," *Reclaiming Children and Youth* 22 (2013): 13–17. Retrieved from https://ezaccess.libraries.psu.edu/login?url=https://www.proquest.com/scholarly-journals/five-shifts-ensuring-environment-healing/docview/1367551506/se-2?accountid=13158.

Chapter Nine: Discovering Your Default Conversation

1. Mary Pipher, *Writing to Change the World: An Inspiring Guide for Transforming the World with Words* (New York: Penguin, 2006), 45–46.

Chapter Eleven: Moving Toward the Greatest Conversation

1. Michael Reeves, *Delighting in the Trinity: An Introduction to the Christian Faith* (Downers Grove, IL: IVP Academic, 2012), 59.

2. Krista Tippett, *Becoming Wise: An Inquiry into the Mystery and Art of Living* (New York: Penguin Press, 2016), 143.

3. Reeves, 51.

What if your ordinary interactions with family, neighbors, and coworkers are actually invitations to adventure with God?

MOODY Publishers

From the Word to Life

Sent will shape your desires, expectations, and confidence to have spiritual conversations that lead others to know Jesus—right where you are. Grow in intimacy with Jesus as you live into your identity as sent.

978-0-8024-1979-8 | also available as an eBook

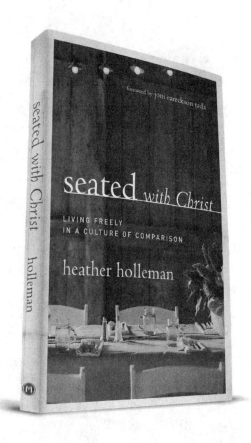